Chuck Williams'

Thanksgiving & Christmas

GENERAL EDITOR
CHUCK WILLIAMS

RECIPES
CHUCK WILLIAMS

PHOTOGRAPHY
ALLAN ROSENBERG

TIME
LIFE
BOOKS

Time-Life Books is a division of
TIME LIFE INCORPORATED

President and CEO: John M. Fahey, Jr.
President, Time-Life Books: John D. Hall

TIME-LIFE CUSTOM PUBLISHING

Vice President and Publisher: Terry Newell
Sales Director: Frances C. Mangan
Editorial Director: Robert A. Doyle

WILLIAMS-SONOMA
Founder/Vice-Chairman: Chuck Williams

WELDON OWEN INC.
President: John Owen
Publisher: Wendely Harvey
Managing Editor: Laurie Wertz
Consulting Editor: Norman Kolpas
Copy Editor: Sharon Silva
Editorial Assistant: Janique Poncelet
Design: John Bull, The Book Design Company
Production: Stephanie Sherman, James Obata,
    Mick Bagnato
Food Photographer: Allan Rosenberg
Additional Food Photography: Allen V. Lott
Primary Food & Prop Stylist: Sandra Griswold
Food Stylist: Heidi Gintner
Assistant Food Stylist: Danielle Di Salvo
Glossary Illustrations: Alice Harth

The Williams-Sonoma Kitchen Library
conceived and produced by Weldon Owen Inc.
814 Montgomery St., San Francisco, CA 94133

In collaboration with Williams-Sonoma
100 North Point, San Francisco, CA 94133

Production by Mandarin Offset, Hong Kong
Printed in Hong Kong

A Note on Weights and Measures:
All recipes include customary U.S. and metric
measurements. Metric conversions are based on
a standard developed for these books and have
been rounded off. Actual weights may vary.

A Weldon Owen Production

Copyright © 1993 Weldon Owen Inc.
Reprinted in 1993; 1994

Library of Congress
Cataloging-in-Publication Data:

Williams, Chuck. [Thanksgiving & Christmas]
    Chuck Williams' Thanksgiving & Christmas /
    general editor, Chuck Williams ; recipes, Chuck Williams ;
    photography, Allan Rosenberg.
        p.   cm. — (Williams-Sonoma
        kitchen library)
    Includes index.
    ISBN 0-7835-0258-3 (trade) ;
    ISBN 0-7835-0259-1 (library)
    1. Thanksgiving cookery. 2. Christmas cookery.
    I. Title.   II. Title: Thanksgiving and Christmas.   III. Series.
TX739.2.T45W55   1993
641.5'68—dc20   93-17988
                                        CIP

Contents

INTRODUCTION

For me, the year is just not complete without the year-end holiday celebrations: a Thanksgiving feast followed a month later by special dinners on both Christmas Eve *and* Christmas Day.

Yet, as I travel around the country talking to Williams-Sonoma's many customers, I am repeatedly surprised at how many people today are insecure about cooking and serving holiday meals. Sure, they remember their grandmothers and mothers successfully doing it. But the knowledge has not always been passed down through the generations.

This book aims to bridge that gap, to show you how easy it can be to organize and prepare festive menus. It begins with the fundamental information you will need, reviewing kitchen equipment, roasting and carving techniques, and basic sauces. Then six of my own favorite holiday menus follow, each one fully illustrated and headed by a brief introduction that offers simple guidelines for preparing the meal with minimum fuss and maximum pleasure.

Those guidelines are the very backbone of this book—the most valuable lessons you can learn. Their goal is to help you get organized. Whichever menu you choose, I strongly urge you to read the recipes thoroughly several weeks in advance. Jot down shopping lists and preparation strategies, making sure to allow plenty of time for buying the best-quality ingredients you can find and doing as much of the work as possible as far in advance as the recipes and your personal schedule permit. This will give you time to plan more efficiently your table settings, decorations and cleanup, so that every aspect of the celebration goes smoothly.

Believe it or not, that's how your mother and grandmother probably made their holiday meals such successes. I am happy to pass the strategies along to you with some of my personal festive recipes—all of them designed to make these celebrations as pleasurable for you, the host, as they are for your guests. Happy holidays!

Chuck Williams

Equipment

Thanksgiving and Christmas meals draw on a wide array of versatile cookware and utensils

A holiday menu calls for the widest range of equipment you are likely to use for any meal. Nevertheless, few if any unusual pieces are required. Everything shown on these pages is a logical addition to any well-stocked kitchen, and will no doubt prove useful during the other ten months of the year as well.

1. Springform Pan
Circular pan with spring-clip side that loosens for easy unmolding of delicate cakes.

2. Food Processor
For chopping, puréeing or mixing.

3. Assorted Kitchen Tools
Crockery jar holds wooden, metal and slotted spoons; basting brush; rubber and wooden spatulas; wire whisk; bulb baster and potato masher.

4. Colander
For draining vegetables and fruits after washing and for straining solids from stock.

5. Tart Pan
Removable bottom of standard 9-inch (23-cm) pan allows tart to be unmolded. Fluted sides give crust an attractive edge.

6. Muffin Tin
For baking standard-sized (about 3½ fl oz/110 ml) popovers or muffins.

7. Metal Pie Pan
Metal—preferably aluminum—conducts heat best for a crisp, browned crust. Standard size is 9 inches (23 cm), measured inside rim.

8. Liquid Measuring Cup
For accurate measuring of liquid ingredients. Choose heavy-duty heat-resistant glass, marked on one side in cups and ounces, on the other in milliliters.

9. Rolling Pin with Handles
The most commonly used rolling pin for pie dough. Choose one with ball-bearing handles for smooth rolling, and a hardwood surface at least 12 inches (30 cm) long. Wider diameter is better for pastry making. To prevent warping, do not wash; wipe clean with a dry cloth.

10. Carving Knives and Forks
The smallest pair carves chickens; the medium-sized pair is for all-purpose use; the longest includes a knife with a scalloped edge, good for carving roast beef and ham.

11. Sharpening Steel
Used regularly, large, rod-shaped steel sharpening tool helps keep kitchen blades finely honed.

12. Cutting Board
Choose one made of tough but resilient white acrylic, which is nonporous and cleans easily. Thoroughly clean the chopping surface after every use.

13. Mushroom Brush
Small, soft-bristled brush gently removes dirt from mushrooms.

14. Steamed Pudding Mold
Stainless-steel mold with water-tight lid, for containing puddings that cook in a water bath.

25. Dry Measuring Cups
In graduated sizes, for precise measuring of dry ingredients.

26. Measuring Spoons
In graduated sizes, for measuring small quantities of ingredients.

27. Kitchen String
For trussing poultry. Choose good-quality linen string, which withstands intense heat with minimal charring.

28. Vegetable Peeler
Curved, slotted swiveling blade thinly strips away peels.

29. Zester
Small, sharp holes at end of stainless-steel blade cut citrus zest into fine shreds.

30. Roasting Thermometers
Standard meat thermometer is inserted into the thickest part of a roast before it goes into the oven. Smaller instant-read thermometer, inserted at the earliest moment the roast might be done, provides a quick and accurate measure.

31. Strainer
For straining solids from stock and draining vegetables.

32. Chef's and Paring Knives
All-purpose chef's knife for chopping and slicing large items or large quantities. Smaller paring knife for peeling vegetables and cutting up small ingredients.

33. Baking Dish
For dressings and side dishes.

34. Skimmer
Wide bowl and fine mesh for efficient removal of froth and scum from surface of stock.

15. Cake and Loaf Pans
For baking cakes and quick breads. Choose good-quality heavy aluminum or tinplate steel, which conducts heat well for fast, even baking.

16. Wire Cooling Rack
Allows air to circulate under baked goods for quick, even cooling.

17. Pastry Blender
For cutting butter or shortening into flour when making pastry by hand.

18. Biscuit Cutter
Stainless-steel tool cuts neat round biscuits.

19. Ricer
Sturdy hinged tool purées softly cooked vegetables by forcing them through fine holes.

20. Nutmeg Grater
Small, fine grater includes a nutmeg storage compartment.

21. Saucepan
For making soups, sauces and small quantities of stock, and for cooking vegetables.

22. Sauté Pan
For general sautéing and for cooking vegetables.

23. Roasting Pans and Racks
Heavy, durable metal pans large enough to hold roasts—the larger one for turkeys, beef rib roasts and legs of lamb; the smaller for chickens and half hams. Sturdy metal racks facilitate lifting and turning, promote more even cooking and prevent sticking.

24. Enameled Saucepan
For general simmering of sauces and cooking of side dishes.

ROASTING

The basics of cooking a holiday main course

Tailor-made for festive main courses, roasting uses the intense, dry heat of an oven to cook whole poultry or large cuts of red meat slowly, for an appetizingly browned surface and tender, juicy interior. Seasonings, added to the body cavity of a turkey or chicken, or rubbed on the surface of a roast, can subtly enhance its flavor. Regular basting promotes browning and moistness.

Cooking time will vary with a roast's size and, for red meats, the desired degree of doneness. Bear in mind, too, that meat put into the oven straight from the refrigerator does not cook evenly and takes longer to roast, so be sure to remove it from the refrigerator beforehand to bring it to room temperature. For accurate roasting temperatures, check your oven in advance by placing a good oven thermometer at its center; adjust oven dial settings accordingly.

Because no two ovens are alike, the roast's internal temperature is your best guide for doneness. Thirty minutes before the estimated completion time, start checking for doneness with an instant-read thermometer; it is more practical and accurate than a regular meat thermometer.

Above all, read these guidelines carefully and plan your menu to allow ample time for roasting. It is always better to have the roast done slightly early than to keep guests waiting.

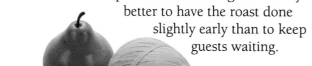

TURKEY

Though some recipes call for roasting at one constant moderate temperature, beginning at a higher temperature helps ensure more even cooking. Starting the bird breast-down yields moister white meat.

✱ Begin roasting breast-side down in a preheated 425°–450°F (220°–230°C) oven for 40 minutes.

✱ Reduce the heat to 325°F (165°C), turn the turkey breast-up, and continue roasting until an instant-read thermometer inserted into the thickest part of the breast, not touching bone, registers 165°F (74°C), or 180°F (82°C) in the thigh. For an 8–12-lb (4–6-kg) turkey, total roasting time will be 2–3¼ hours. For a 12–16-lb (6–8-kg) turkey, 3¼–4¼ hours. For a 16–20-lb (8–10-kg) turkey, 4¼–5 hours.

✱ For a stuffed turkey, add 30–45 minutes to total roasting time.

TURKEY BREAST

A foil shield keeps the skin from browning too fast.

✱ Roast skin-side up, loosely covered with foil, in a preheated 350°F (180°C) oven for 50 minutes.

✱ Uncover and continue roasting until golden brown; remove from the oven when an instant-read thermometer inserted into its thickest part, not touching bone, registers 165°–170°F (74°–77°C). For a 4–6-lb (2–3-kg) bone-in breast, total roasting time will be 1¼–1½ hours; for a 6–8-lb (3–4-kg) bone-in breast, 1½–2 hours.

LEG OF LAMB

Roasting at a moderate temperature safeguards the succulence of a leg of lamb's tender meat.

✱ Roast in a preheated 350°F (180°C) oven until browned and cooked to the desired doneness.

✱ For rare to medium-rare, roast until an instant-read thermometer inserted into its thickest part, not touching bone, registers 135°–140°F (57°–60°C), about 1½ hours for a 6–7-lb (3–3.5-kg) leg. For medium, roast until a thermometer registers 150°F (65°C), about 2 hours.

Prime Rib of Beef

The initial high-heat roasting sears the beef's surface; subsequent roasting at a lower temperature cooks the meat evenly and keeps it moist.

✱ Begin roasting rib-side down in a preheated 500°F (260°C) oven for 15 minutes.

✱ Reduce the heat to 325°F (165°C) and continue roasting until the meat is browned and reaches the desired degree of doneness.

✱ For rare, roast until an instant-read thermometer inserted into its center, not touching bone, registers 120°F (50°C), about 15 minutes per pound (500 g). For medium, roast until a thermometer registers 135°F (57°C), about 20 minutes per pound (500 g).

Chicken

A low roasting temperature helps keep chicken moist and succulent. For even roasting, start the chicken on one side, turn it to the other side, then finish it breast-side up.

✱ Roast in a preheated 325°F (165°C) oven until golden brown, removing it when an instant-read thermometer inserted into the thickest part of the thigh, not touching bone, registers 180°F (82°C). For a 2–4-lb (1–2-kg) chicken, total roasting time will be 1–1½ hours. For a 4–7-lb (2–3.5-kg) chicken, 1½–2 hours.

✱ For a stuffed chicken, add 20–30 minutes to total roasting time.

Ham

Partially cooked hams, usually labeled "cook before eating," require only simple cooking in an open pan before serving.

✱ Bake a bone-in, partially cooked ham in a preheated 350°F (180°C) oven until an instant-read thermometer inserted into its thickest part, not touching bone, registers 160°F (70°C), about 12 minutes per pound (500 g)— 2–2½ hours for a 10–12-lb (5–6-kg) ham.

Trussing

Tying, or trussing, whole turkeys or chickens into a compact shape helps ensure they cook more evenly, and yields a roast bird that is not only more attractive to present at table but also neater and easier to carve.

There are many different methods for trussing. The one demonstrated below is among the easiest. It employs a single piece of string that is at least long enough to wrap twice lengthwise around the bird; the longer the piece of string you use, the easier it will be to pull tight. Choose a good, sturdy linen kitchen string, which is less likely to scorch in the heat of the oven.

If you've stuffed the bird, handle it carefully to make sure nothing spills out, holding the neck flap securely shut as you complete the trussing.

1. Securing the drumsticks.
With the bird breast-side up, slide the center of the string under its tail. Cross the ends above the tail and loop them around the drumsticks; then cross them again and pull them tight to draw together the tail and the ends of the drumsticks.

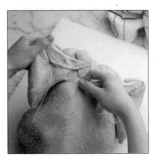

2. Securing the wings.
Turn the bird over. Tuck the wing tips across the neck flap. Pull one string end along the side, loop it around the nearest wing, pull it tight across the neck flap and loop it around the other wing. Tie the two string ends tightly together. Cut off excess string.

CARVING

Simple steps yield perfect serving slices from a holiday roast

Carving roast poultry or meat for the holiday table is too often regarded as a skill requiring years of practice to master. In fact, provided you have the proper tools and understand the basic shape of the roast at hand, carving turkey, chicken, ham, beef or lamb can be a simple, even pleasurable task.

A good, sharp slicing knife and a two-pronged fork to steady the roast are essential (see pages 6–7). While an all-purpose slicing knife may be used for carving any type of roast, different knives are better suited to some roasts than to others. One with a long, flexible but still sturdy blade is best for following the contours of a large turkey. A shorter, sturdier knife makes quicker, smoother work of the smaller chicken. Long, straight blades with scalloped edges cut more readily through red meats. Whatever knife you use, make sure it is well-sharpened for easier, safer carving.

TURKEY

Generous in size, a turkey offers each guest an ample choice of dark leg meat and white breast meat. Carve only as much as you need to serve at one time, completing one side before starting the next.

1. Remove the leg and wing.
With the turkey breast up, cut through the skin between thigh and breast. Move the leg to locate the thigh joint, then cut through the joint to sever the leg. In the same way, remove the wing (shown at left), cutting through the shoulder joint where it meets the breast.

2. Slice the drumstick and thigh.
Cut through the joint to separate the drumstick and thigh. Serve them whole; or carve, cutting the meat into thin slices parallel to their bones.

3. Carve the breast.
Just above the thigh and shoulder joints, carve a deep horizontal cut toward the bone, creating a base cut on one side of the breast. Starting near the breastbone, carve thin slices vertically, cutting parallel to the rib cage and ending at the base cut.

CHICKEN

The basics of carving a chicken are similar to those for turkey. But because of the bird's smaller size, the drumstick and the thigh can be served whole and, depending upon the number of guests, the entire chicken may be carved at once.

1. Remove the leg and wing.
With the chicken breast up, cut through the skin between thigh and breast. Move the leg to locate the thigh joint, then cut through the joint to sever the leg (shown at left). In the same way, remove the wing, cutting through the shoulder joint where it meets the breast.

2. Separate the drumstick and thigh.
If the chicken is small, serve the whole leg as an individual portion. If it is larger, cut through the joint to separate the drumstick and thigh into two pieces. You may want to slice a large thigh into two pieces.

3. Carve the breast.
Starting at the breastbone, cut downward and parallel to the rib cage, carving the meat into long, thin slices.

HAM

Whether you are carving a whole ham or a butt or shank end, the carving process is basically the same: cutting parallel slices perpendicular to the bone, which are then freed by cutting horizontally along the bone.

1. Cut the first slice.
Place the ham—here, a bone-in butt end—on a carving surface. Starting at its widest end, cut a vertical slice about ¼ inch (6 mm) thick and perpendicular to the bone.

2. Cut parallel slices.
Continue making cuts of the same width and parallel to the first, cutting as many slices as you wish to serve.

3. Free the slices from the bone.
To free the slices, cut horizontally through their base, with the knife blade parallel to the bone. When all the meat has been removed from the first side, turn the ham over and repeat on the second side.

11

BEEF

A prime rib of beef is fairly simple to carve, provided you have a large, sharp knife for slicing and a sturdy fork to steady the roast. You might wish to leave some slices attached to the ribs, for guests who prefer the meat on the bone.

1. Cut the first slice. Place the roast, ribs down, on a carving surface and steady it by inserting a carving fork. Using a long, sharp, sturdy blade, cut a vertical slice across the grain from one end of the roast down to the rib bone, cutting along the bone to free the slice.

2. Continue carving. Cutting parallel to the first slice, continue to carve slices of the desired thickness. As individual rib bones are exposed, cut between them to remove them; or leave them attached to slices for guests who request them.

LAMB

Shaped like an irregular, elongated pear, a leg of lamb presents a challenge to the carver. The keys to successful carving lie in cutting parallel to the bone and providing guests with slices from both sides of the leg.

1. Slice the rounded side. Firmly grasp the protruding end of the shank bone with a kitchen towel and tilt it slightly upward. Using a long, sharp, sturdy knife, carve a first slice from the rounded, meaty side of the leg at its widest point, cutting away from you and roughly parallel to the bone.

2. Cut parallel slices. Cutting parallel to the first slice, continue carving the meat in thin slices until you have cut enough to give each guest a slice.

3. Carve the inner side. Grasping the bone, rotate the leg of lamb to expose its other, flatter side—the inner side of the leg, which is slightly more tender. Still cutting parallel to the bone, carve a slice of this meat for each guest.

Chicken or Turkey Stock

To prepare the dressing and gravy for roasted chicken or turkey, you will need good stock. If you make chicken stock occasionally and store it in the freezer, so much the better. If not, make this stock a few days in advance and refrigerate it tightly covered. This recipe yields more than enough stock for making both the gravy and dressing for a dinner serving 8–10 persons. The remainder can be used for making soup or other dishes. Use the cooked chicken or turkey meat for a salad or casserole.

2 lb (1 kg) chicken wings or turkey wings or other parts
8 cups (64 fl oz/2 l) water
2 celery stalks, cut into pieces
1 yellow onion, quartered
1 bay leaf
2 or 3 fresh thyme sprigs or ½ teaspoon crushed
   dried thyme
3 large fresh parsley sprigs
2 lemon peel strips, each 2 inches (5 cm) long and
   ½ inch (12 mm) wide
2 teaspoons salt, or to taste

Rinse the poultry parts and place in a large saucepan with the water. Bring to a boil over high heat, regularly skimming off the froth from the surface. Reduce the heat to a simmer and add the celery, onion, bay leaf, thyme, parsley, lemon peel and salt. Cover partially and simmer until the meat is falling from the bones, about 1½ hours.

Remove from the heat and strain. Let the stock cool, then refrigerate it in a container with a tight-fitting lid. Just before using, lift off the fat from the surface of the stock. You should have at least 6 cups stock. If there is less, add water as needed.

Makes 6–7 cups (48–56 fl oz/1.5–1.75 l)

BASIC STEPS FOR CHICKEN OR TURKEY STOCK

Long, gentle simmering extracts the essence from poultry, aromatic vegetables and herbs to make a basic stock. Diligent skimming ensures a clean-tasting, clear liquid.

1. Filling the stockpot. Place chicken or turkey parts in a large stockpot or saucepan. Alternatively, use a small whole chicken. Add cold water to cover completely.

2. Skimming the stock. Bring the liquid to a boil while regularly skimming off froth and scum from the surface with a skimmer. When the stock gently boils, reduce the heat, add vegetables and seasonings, cover partially and simmer about 1½ hours.

3. Straining and degreasing. Pour the stock through a strainer into a bowl. Let the stock cool to room temperature, then cover and refrigerate. Using a large spoon, skim the solidified fat from its surface.

Chicken or Turkey Gravy

Be sure to measure all the ingredients in advance, so the gravy can be made quickly just before serving. For added flavor, stir in 1 or 2 tablespoons sherry at the last minute. I have found that a large quantity of gravy is needed for holiday dinners, especially when serving mashed potatoes and dressing.

¼ cup (2 fl oz/60 ml) dry white wine
¼ cup (2 fl oz/60 ml) water
5 tablespoons all-purpose (plain) flour
4 cups (32 fl oz/1 l) chicken or turkey stock, heated
  (*recipe on page 13*)
salt and freshly ground pepper

After removing the chicken or turkey from the roasting pan, skim or pour off the fat from the pan juices, reserving 3–4 tablespoons of the fat. To the remaining pan juices, add the wine and the water and place over medium heat. Bring to a boil and boil for 2–3 minutes, stirring with a wooden spoon to dislodge any browned bits stuck to the bottom of the pan. Strain into a bowl and set aside.

In a saucepan over medium heat, warm the reserved fat until it is bubbly. Add the flour and stir rapidly for a few seconds to cook the flour. Add the strained pan juices and 3½ cups (28 fl oz/875 ml) of the stock. Cook, while rapidly stirring, until smooth and thickened, 1–2 minutes. Add the remaining stock as needed to achieve the desired gravy consistency.

Season to taste with salt and pepper. Pour into a warmed sauceboat and serve.

Makes about 4 cups (32 fl oz/1 l)

BASIC STEPS FOR MAKING GRAVY

Gravy is made while a turkey or chicken rests before carving. Take care to sprinkle and stir the flour well to prevent it from forming lumps.

1. Deglazing the pan. Skim or pour off all the fat from the pan juices in the roasting pan; reserve 3–4 tablespoons of the fat. Add wine and water to the pan, place over medium heat and stir and scrape to dislodge the pan deposits. Strain the liquid and set it aside.

2. Cooking the flour. Warm the reserved fat in a saucepan over medium heat. Sprinkle in the flour and stir rapidly to cook it, breaking up any lumps.

3. Finishing the gravy. Stir in the strained pan juices and the stock. Cook, stirring continuously, for 1 minute. Add more stock, if necessary, to achieve a thick but still fairly liquid consistency. Season to taste before serving.

Apple-Mint Chutney

This is an excellent accompaniment to lamb, poultry or pork. Also try serving it with your favorite curried chicken or lamb. Look for a good French Champagne vinegar for the best results. And by all means use fresh mint if possible.

1 small red bell pepper (capsicum)
3 large tart apples such as Granny Smith, McIntosh or Rome
¾ cup (4 oz/125 g) golden raisins
1 cup (7 oz/220 g) firmly packed light brown sugar
½ cup (4 fl oz/125 ml) Champagne vinegar or other white wine vinegar
3 tablespoons minced fresh mint or 1 tablespoon crushed dried mint

Roast the bell pepper as directed in the glossary, page 104. Pull off the loosened skin and remove the core, seeds and ribs. Cut the pepper into ¼-inch (6-mm) dice. You should have about ½ cup (3 oz/90 g); set aside.

Peel, quarter and core the apples. Slice each quarter in half again lengthwise and then cut into ½-inch (12-mm) chunks. Put into a heavy enameled or stainless-steel saucepan. Add the raisins, sugar and vinegar. Bring just to a boil over high heat. Reduce the heat to a simmer and cook slowly, uncovered, stirring several times, until the apples are tender and the juice reduces and thickens, 45–60 minutes.

Add the mint and reserved bell pepper. Stir well and cook for 2–3 minutes longer. The apples should be translucent and the mixture should have a thick consistency.

Let cool to room temperature and serve. Or cover and refrigerate for up to 2–3 days; bring to room temperature before serving.

Makes about 2½ cups (1½ lb/750 g)

Cranberry Horseradish Sauce

This makes a small amount of horseradish sauce for serving with roast beef or other meats and poultry. It is best to use the freshly grated prepared horseradish found in jars in the refrigerated section of food markets. The sauce may be prepared, covered and refrigerated for up to 24 hours before serving.

2 cups (8 oz/250 g) fresh cranberries
¼ cup (2 oz/60 g) sugar
⅓ cup (3 oz/90 g) prepared horseradish

Sort the cranberries, discarding any soft ones. Finely chop them and put into a small saucepan with the sugar. Heat over medium heat, stirring constantly until the sugar dissolves and the mixture is fully blended, about 2 minutes. It does not need to cook. Set aside to cool. Stir in the horseradish and serve.

Makes about 1 cup (10 oz/315 g)

Minted Cranberry Sauce

Fresh mint adds a pleasant flavor to cranberries. You will need 12–14 large mint sprigs; use the leaves only. This can be made a day in advance, covered and refrigerated. Although I like to serve it with chicken or turkey, this sprightly sauce is also good with lamb or ham.

⅓ cup (½ oz/15 g) firmly packed coarsely chopped
   fresh mint leaves
⅓ cup (3 fl oz/80 ml) boiling water
4 cups (1 lb/500 g) fresh cranberries
1 cup (8 oz/250 g) sugar
⅔ cup (5 fl oz/160 ml) cold water
finely shredded zest of ½ lemon

Place the mint in a small bowl and pour in the boiling water. Let steep for 10–15 minutes. Sort the cranberries, discarding any soft ones.

   Combine the sugar and cold water in a saucepan. Bring to a boil, stirring to dissolve the sugar completely. Add the cranberries and lemon zest. Return to a boil, reduce the heat to a simmer, cover partially and cook until thickened and the cranberries have burst, about 10 minutes.

   Using a fine-mesh sieve placed over a glass measuring cup, strain the mint leaves, pressing them with the back of a spoon to release all the flavored water; you should have about ¼ cup (2 fl oz/60 ml) liquid. Add it to the cranberries, stir well to blend and cook for 1 minute more.

   Pour into a bowl and let cool before serving. Or cover tightly and refrigerate; bring to room temperature before serving.

   Makes about 2¼ cups (1½ lb/750 g)

Apple-Orange Cranberry Sauce

A variation on the traditional cranberry sauce, this flavorful blend is excellent with poultry or almost any meat, hot or cold. It can be made a day in advance and refrigerated in a covered container.

½ orange
2 cups (16 fl oz/500 ml) water
1 tart apple such as Granny Smith, pippin or McIntosh
3 cups (12 oz/375 g) fresh cranberries
1¼ cups (10 oz/310 g) sugar
½ teaspoon ground cinnamon
¼ teaspoon ground cloves

Squeeze the juice from the orange half and set the juice aside. Remove the membrane from the inside of the orange shell and discard. Cut the shell into small dice. Put into a small saucepan with the water, bring to a boil and cook for 10 minutes. Drain and set aside.

Peel, quarter and core the apple, then chop into small pieces. Place in a saucepan. Sort the cranberries, discarding any soft ones. Add to the apples along with the reserved diced orange peel, the reserved orange juice, the sugar, cinnamon and cloves. Bring to a boil, reduce the heat to a simmer and cover partially. Simmer gently, stirring occasionally, until the sauce has thickened, the apple is tender and the cranberries have burst, 10–15 minutes.

Transfer to a bowl and let cool before serving. Or cover and refrigerate; bring to room temperature before serving.

Makes 3½–4 cups (2¼–2½ lb/1–1.25 kg)

Poached Orange Slices

The thin-skinned, seedless navel orange is the best for poaching. The slices can be made a day ahead and refrigerated in their liquid in a covered container. Serve with baked ham, chicken or poached fruit.

1 or 2 small thin-skinned oranges
1 cup (8 oz/250 g) sugar
2 cups (16 fl oz/500 ml) water

Cut each unpeeled orange crosswise into 7 or 8 thin slices, discarding the end pieces and any seeds. Fill a sauté pan or frying pan half full with water and bring to a boil. Add the orange slices and cook for 1 minute. Drain and set aside.

In the same pan combine the sugar and the water. Bring to a boil, stirring to dissolve the sugar completely. Reduce the heat to medium-low, add the orange slices and gently cook uncovered, turning a couple of times, until tender, about 5 minutes. Set the slices aside to cool in their liquid.

Makes 7 or 8 slices per orange

Tart and Pie Pastry

Vegetable shortening makes a flaky pastry; butter results in a richer, crispier pastry. One can be substituted successfully for the other, however.

FOR ONE 9- OR 10-INCH (23- OR 25-CM) TART SHELL:
1½ cups (7½ oz/235 g) all-purpose (plain) flour
1 tablespoon sugar
¼ teaspoon salt
½ cup (4 oz/125 g) unsalted butter, chilled, cut into
  small cubes
3–4 tablespoons ice water

FOR ONE 9-INCH (23-CM) DOUBLE-CRUST PIE:
2½ cups (12½ oz/390 g) all-purpose (plain) flour
1 tablespoon sugar
½ teaspoon salt
¾ cup (6 oz/180 g) vegetable shortening
6–7 tablespoons cold water

To make the dough by hand, in a bowl stir together the flour, sugar and salt. Add the butter or shortening and, using a pastry blender, fingertips or 2 knives, cut the butter or shortening into the flour until crumbly and the mixture resembles oatmeal. Then, while quickly stirring and tossing with a fork, add the water, a little at a time, until the dough forms a loose ball.

  To make the dough in a food processor, place the flour, sugar and salt in the work bowl fitted with the metal blade. Pulse a few times to blend. Add the butter or shortening and process with on-off pulses until crumbly and the mixture resembles oatmeal. Add half of the water with a few short pulses and then the remaining water as needed, pulsing 2 or 3 more times until the mixture starts to hold together. Feel the dough; it should mass together between your fingers. Add a little more water if necessary. Gather into a ball.

  Form the dough into a single flat, round cake, or for the double-crust pie, into 2 cakes, one slightly larger than the other. Cover with plastic wrap and refrigerate for at least 30 minutes, or for up to 2 hours.

Makes pastry for one 9- or 10-inch (23- or 25-cm) tart shell or one 9-inch (23-cm) double-crust pie

Lemon Whipped Cream

To make this rich yet refreshing topping, use regular heavy whipping cream with a short expiration date, not the ultrapasteurized cream with a long shelf life that can be difficult to whip. Adding a little sour cream contributes a bit of flavor and aids in thickening. This cream is a wonderful accompaniment to fruit or custard pies, cobblers, cooked fruit, custards or puddings.

1 cup (8 fl oz/250 ml) heavy (double) cream
2 tablespoons sour cream
2 tablespoons confectioners' (icing) sugar
1 tablespoon fresh lemon juice
finely grated zest of 1 lemon

In a bowl combine the heavy cream and sour cream. Using a whisk or electric mixer, beat until the mixture begins to thicken. Add the sugar and lemon juice and zest. Continue beating only until soft folds form. Do not beat too stiff.

  The cream can be covered and refrigerated for up to 3 hours. Stir well before using.

Makes about 2 cups (16 fl oz/500 ml)

Ginger or Orange Sabayon Cream

Flavoring this whipped cream sauce with either ginger or orange produces equally delicious results. Use regular heavy whipping cream, not the ultrapasteurized kind that can be difficult to whip. This sauce is excellent with steamed puddings, gingerbread, poached fruit and fruit breads. It can be made several hours ahead, and leftover sauce can be covered and refrigerated for up to 2 days.

3 egg yolks
¼ cup (2 oz/60 g) granulated sugar
1 teaspoon finely grated fresh ginger, or the finely grated zest of 1 orange and 1 tablespoon fresh orange juice
1 cup (8 fl oz/250 ml) heavy (double) cream
1 tablespoon confectioners' (icing) sugar

Have ready a pan of ice mixed with a little water. In a heatproof bowl placed over a saucepan of barely simmering water (not touching bowl), whisk together the egg yolks and granulated sugar. Add the ginger or the orange zest and orange juice. Using a whisk or electric mixer, beat until light colored and thickened, 5–6 minutes. Remove the bowl from the heat and nest it in the ice water. Continue whisking until cold. It will get quite thick. Set aside.

In another bowl whip the cream until soft folds form. Add the confectioners' sugar and whip until stiff peaks form. Stir the cream into the egg yolk mixture just until blended and smooth. Cover and refrigerate. Stir well before serving, as it may separate slightly upon sitting.

Makes about 2½–3 cups (20–24 fl oz/625–750 ml)

Brandy Butter Sauce

This is a lighter version of the traditional brandy sauce that is usually served with plum pudding. It complements any warm steamed pudding and can be made several hours in advance.

4 egg yolks
¼ cup (2 fl oz/60 ml) good brandy or Cognac
2 teaspoons fresh lemon juice
½ cup (4 oz/125 g) granulated sugar
½ cup (4 oz/125 g) unsalted butter, cut into small cubes
½ cup (4 fl oz/125 ml) heavy (double) cream
1 tablespoon confectioners' (icing) sugar

Have ready a large bowl three-fourths full with ice and a little water. Pour water into a small saucepan to a depth of 1 inch (2.5 cm) and bring just to a simmer.

In a bowl (which will eventually rest over but not touch the simmering water) whisk together the egg yolks, brandy, lemon juice and granulated sugar. Place over the saucepan of simmering water and whisk vigorously until thickened and doubled in volume, 6–7 minutes.

Remove the bowl from the heat and beat in the butter, a little at a time, until dissolved and blended. Immediately nest the bowl in the ice water and continue beating until cold and quite thick, 6–8 minutes.

In another bowl whip the cream until soft folds form. Add the confectioners' sugar and whip until stiff peaks form. Using a rubber spatula fold the cream into the yolk mixture. Cover and refrigerate. Serve cold.

Makes about 2½ cups (20 fl oz/625 ml)

All the long-cherished elements of Thanksgiving are present in this menu. Yet, I've also included some up-to-date touches, such as the light first-course salad, the herb seasonings for the turkey, the addition of parsnips to the mashed potatoes, and the vinaigrette dressing that replaces the heavier butter sauce usually served on green beans and onions. And I've added a lively orange flavor to the traditional pumpkin pie.

As you'll see, I prefer to bake the stuffing separately, which prevents it from turning soggy and reduces the roasting time of the bird. If your taste runs to a moister stuffing, by all means bake it inside the bird, increasing the roasting time accordingly (see page 8).

To help make the meal go as smoothly as possible, I suggest you read through all the recipes well in advance, jotting down shopping lists and double-checking that you have all the necessary equipment. The day before the meal, you could make the cranberry sauce; make and bake the pastry crust for the tart; prepare the dressing's bread crumbs and the bell pepper for the green beans; and wash the salad greens, refrigerating them to chill and crisp.

Don't forget a good white or light red wine for the holiday toasts.

A Traditional Thanksgiving

★

Orange and Avocado Salad with
Honey-Mint Dressing

Herbed Roast Turkey with Gravy

Baked Chestnut and Ham Dressing

Apple-Orange Cranberry Sauce
(recipe on page 17)

Mashed Potatoes with Parsnips

Green Beans and Pearl Onions
with Tarragon Vinaigrette

Pumpkin-Orange Tart with
Orange Sabayon Cream

Serves 8–10

Orange and Avocado Salad

½–¾ lb (250–375 g) baby salad spinach, carefully washed and trimmed

2 or 3 ripe avocados, depending upon size

4 or 5 medium-to-large oranges, preferably seedless

3 tablespoons fresh lemon juice

½ teaspoon salt

¼ cup (3 oz/90 g) honey, preferably mild flavored

freshly ground pepper

½ cup (4 fl oz/125 ml) mild extra-virgin olive oil

2 tablespoons minced sweet red (Spanish) onion or green (spring) onion

1½ teaspoons minced fresh mint leaves or 1 teaspoon crushed dried mint

Grapefruit can be substituted for the oranges, and watercress can stand in for the spinach leaves. Look for baby spinach that has already been washed and dried for use in salads. It can be found in the vegetable section of better food markets. All the components of the salad can be prepared up to 2–3 hours in advance and assembled at the last moment. If cutting the avocado in advance, sprinkle with lemon juice to prevent it from discoloring.

★

Wrap the spinach in a clean, damp kitchen towel. Place in the refrigerator for at least 2–3 hours to chill and crisp.

Cut each avocado in half, remove the pit and then peel. Cut lengthwise into thin slices; set aside. Peel the oranges; remove any remaining white membrane covering them and then cut crosswise into thin slices, discarding any seeds. Set aside.

In a small bowl stir together the lemon juice and salt until the salt dissolves. Whisk in the honey and a little pepper, then whisk in the olive oil, onion and mint. Taste and adjust the seasoning. Set aside.

To assemble, arrange the chilled spinach on individual plates. Top with avocado slices and orange slices. Whisk the dressing again and drizzle over the salad, or pass it separately in a bowl.

Serves 8–10

Herbed Roast Turkey

12–14 lb (6–7 kg) turkey, at room
 temperature
1 yellow onion, quartered
2 celery stalks, cut into 2-inch (5-cm)
 lengths
3 or 4 fresh parsley sprigs
1 bay leaf
1 tablespoon dried sage
2 teaspoons dried thyme
2 teaspoons dried marjoram
salt and freshly ground pepper
6 tablespoons (3 oz/90 g) unsalted
 butter, melted

*Seek out a fresh rather than a frozen turkey. Remove from the
refrigerator 1 hour before roasting, to bring to room temperature. Offer
apple-orange cranberry sauce (recipe on page 17) at the table.*

★

Preheat an oven to 425°F (220°C). Position a rack in the bottom
third of the oven. Oil a V-shaped rack in a roasting pan.

Remove the neck, gizzard and heart from the turkey, if included;
reserve for another use. Rinse the bird in cold water and pat dry
with paper towels. Place the onion, celery, parsley and bay leaf in
the cavity. In a small bowl mix together the sage, thyme and
marjoram. Place 2 teaspoons of the mixture in the cavity, then
sprinkle with salt and pepper. Truss the turkey, if desired (see page
9); brush with some of the butter and sprinkle, especially the breast
and thighs, with the remaining herb mixture and salt and pepper.

Place on the rack in the pan, breast-side down. Roast for 40
minutes, basting with butter after 20 minutes. Reduce the heat to
325°F (165°C), turn breast-side up and continue to roast, basting
with the remaining butter until used up and then with the pan
juices every 15–20 minutes. Roast until golden and cooked
through. After about 2½ hours, start testing for doneness by
inserting an instant-read thermometer in the thickest part of the
breast away from the bone; it should register 165°F (74°C).
Alternatively, insert it in the thickest part of the thigh; it should
register 180°F (82°C). The turkey should roast a total of about
3½ hours or 15–17 minutes per pound (500 g); see page 8.

Transfer to a warmed platter and cover loosely with aluminum
foil until ready to carve, about 20 minutes. Meanwhile, use the pan
juices to make the gravy (recipe on page 14). Carve the turkey (see
page 10) and serve with the gravy.

Serves 8–10

Baked Chestnut and Ham Dressing

1 large loaf French or Italian bread,
   about 1¼ lb (625 g)
2 tablespoons unsalted butter
2 cups (10 oz/315 g) diced yellow onion
½ lb (250 g) cooked ham, fat trimmed
   and coarsely chopped
1½ cups (½ lb/250 g) diced celery
1 cup (5 oz/155 g) diced red bell pepper
   (capsicum)
2 teaspoons crushed dried sage
2 cups (16 fl oz/500 ml) chicken stock
   or turkey stock, preferably homemade
   (*recipe on page 13*)
1 lb (500 g) chestnuts, peeled and
   chopped (*see glossary, page 104*)
3–4 tablespoons chopped fresh parsley
salt and freshly ground pepper

It is much easier to bake dressing separately. It has better texture and flavor when baked in a dish rather than "steamed" inside the bird. If you do not have two ovens, start the dressing in the 325°F (165°C) oven with the turkey. When the turkey is removed and set aside to rest before carving, increase the oven temperature to 375°F (190°C) to finish baking the dressing. The cooking time may need to be increased slightly. Prepare the bread crumbs the night before so they can dry overnight. Purchase a freshly cut ham slice about ⅜ inch (9 mm) thick from a good meat market or a butcher in the meat department of a quality supermarket. You can use the roasted and peeled chestnuts packed in jars, if you like.

★

*T*he night before, slice or tear the bread, including the crusts, into small pieces. Place in a food processor fitted with the metal blade and process to form coarse crumbs. (You should have about 12 cups.) Spread out the crumbs on large baking sheets or newspapers to dry overnight.

Preheat an oven to 375°F (190°C). Butter a 3-qt (3-l) baking dish. In a large sauté pan or frying pan over medium heat, melt the butter. Add the onion and cook gently, stirring occasionally, until translucent, 2–3 minutes. Add the ham, celery, bell pepper and sage. Mix well and cook for another 2 minutes. Set aside.

Place the bread crumbs in a large bowl. While rapidly tossing and stirring the crumbs, gradually add the stock; the crumbs should be evenly moistened. Add the sautéed vegetables, the chestnuts, parsley and salt and pepper to taste. (Remember the stock may have been seasoned and ham is salty.) Mix and toss until well blended.

Spoon loosely into the prepared baking dish. Place in the oven and bake until golden on top, 40–50 minutes.

Serves 8–10

Mashed Potatoes with Parsnips

4 lb (2 kg) potatoes, peeled and cut into
   1½-inch (4-cm) chunks
1 lb (500 g) parsnips, peeled and cut
   into 1-inch (2.5-cm) chunks
1 tablespoon salt, plus salt for seasoning
½–¾ cup (4–6 fl oz/125–180 ml) milk,
   warmed
freshly ground pepper
chopped fresh parsley, optional

A few parsnips cooked and mashed with potatoes give the potatoes a sweeter flavor and smoother texture. It is important they be mashed by hand with a potato masher or put through a ricer. Do not use a food processor, as it will make the potatoes gluey. This dish is very rich on its own; a pat of butter makes it even more so.

★

*P*ut the potatoes and parsnips into a large saucepan and add water to cover. Add the 1 tablespoon salt, cover partially and bring to a boil over high heat. Reduce the heat to medium-low and boil gently until tender when pierced with a fork, 20–25 minutes. Drain well.

Mash the potatoes and parsnips together with a potato masher, or put them through a ricer, until free of all lumps. Then, while gradually adding the milk, beat with a wooden spoon until smooth and fluffy. Add only as much of the milk as needed to achieve the desired consistency.

Season to taste with salt and pepper. Beat over medium heat until very hot. Spoon into a warmed serving dish and garnish with parsley, if desired.

Serves 8–10

Green Beans and Pearl Onions with Tarragon Vinaigrette

1 red bell pepper (capsicum)

12–14 oz (375–440 g) pearl onions, about ¾ inch (2 cm) in diameter, unpeeled

3 tablespoons salt, plus pinch of salt

2 lb (1 kg) fresh green beans, preferably Blue Lake

1–2 tablespoons tarragon white wine vinegar

5 tablespoons (3 fl oz/80 ml) extra-virgin olive oil

freshly ground pepper

Look for young, tender beans. If they are limp, immerse them in ice water for 30 minutes before cooking. Use a high-quality tarragon-flavored white wine vinegar. Champagne vinegar from France is best.

★

Roast the bell pepper as directed in the glossary, page 104. Pull off the loosened skin and remove the core, seeds and ribs. Cut the pepper into long, thin strips. Set aside.

Fill a saucepan three-fourths full with water and bring to a boil. Add the onions and 1 tablespoon of the salt and bring back to a boil. Reduce the heat slightly, cover partially and cook for 2–3 minutes; drain and plunge into cold water. Cut off the root ends; trim the stems if you like. Slip off skins and set the onions aside.

Trim off the stems from the green beans and cut the beans into 3-inch (7.5-cm) lengths. Bring a large saucepan of water to a boil. Add the remaining 2 tablespoons salt and the beans. Bring back to a rapid boil and cook, uncovered, until just tender but still crisp, about 5 minutes. Drain immediately and plunge into ice water to stop the cooking and to cool. Drain again and set aside.

Just before serving, combine 1 tablespoon of the vinegar and the pinch of salt in a small bowl and stir to dissolve the salt. Add the olive oil, then pepper to taste and whisk together. Pour into a saucepan and warm over medium heat. Add the bell pepper, onions and beans and toss until heated through, 1 minute. Taste for seasoning, adding more vinegar or salt if needed.

Serves 8–10

Pumpkin-Orange Tart

pastry for a 10-inch (25-cm) tart *(recipe on page 18)*

⅓ cup (4 oz/125 g) orange marmalade

1¾ cups (1 lb/500 g) pumpkin purée

¾ cup (6 oz/185 g) sugar

finely grated zest of 1 orange

½ teaspoon ground cloves

¼ teaspoon ground ginger

½ teaspoon ground allspice

½ teaspoon salt

3 eggs, lightly beaten

1 cup (8 fl oz/250 ml) heavy (double) cream

orange sabayon cream *(recipe on page 19)*

Prebaking the crust ensures a crisp, flaky pastry. Use a 9-inch (23-cm) pie pan if you like; the pie must be served from the pan, however.

★

On a lightly floured surface, roll out the pastry dough into a 13-inch (33-cm) round. Fit into a 10-inch (25-cm) round fluted tart pan with removable bottom. There should be approximately 1 inch (2.5 cm) overhang. Fold over the excess dough. Press it against the sides to make them thicker and build them higher than the pan rim by about ⅜ inch (9 mm). The shell should be about 1¼ inches (3 cm) deep to accommodate the filling. Prick the bottom a few times with the tines of a fork. Prepare a double thickness of aluminum foil large enough to line the tart shell generously. Poke a couple holes in it, carefully fit it into the shell and fold the excess over the rim. Refrigerate for 20–30 minutes.

Meanwhile, preheat an oven to 425°F (220°C). Place the orange marmalade in a small saucepan over low heat until melted. Set aside.

Remove the pastry shell from the refrigerator and bake for 10 minutes. Remove the foil and continue to bake until lightly golden, another 10–12 minutes. If the bottom puffs up during baking, prick it with a fork. Transfer to a cooling rack. Brush the inside bottom and sides with the melted marmalade. Let cool.

In a bowl stir together the pumpkin, sugar, orange zest, cloves, ginger, allspice and salt. Mix in the eggs and then the cream until smooth. Pour into the tart shell and smooth the top. Bake for 15 minutes. Reduce the heat to 325°F (165°C) and bake until a knife inserted in the center comes out clean, about 35 minutes longer.

Cool on a wire rack. Remove the pan sides and place the tart on a serving plate. Serve with the orange sabayon cream.

Serves 8–10

Nobody ever said you *had* to have a turkey on the Thanksgiving table. In fact, none of the historical accounts of the first Thanksgiving actually mention that bird—only that "fowle" was served. So this roast chicken dinner, full of light, fresh flavors and bright colors, strikes me as perfectly appropriate. And it has the added benefit of being well suited to entertaining throughout the year.

With such versatility in mind, I took special care to make sure this menu was easy to prepare and serve. Many things can be done the day before: cooking the potatoes and roasting the peppers for the salad, and washing and crisping the greens in the refrigerator; making and drying the bread crumbs for the dressing; making the cranberry sauce; toasting the almonds for the broccoli; and poaching the fruit for the dessert. Don't forget to raise the oven temperature and bake the biscuits after you take the roast chicken out of the oven to rest before carving.

Be sure to order the chicken in advance from a good food market or poultry shop, to ensure that you get the best-quality bird. The fresh "free-range" chickens found today are excellent. You may have to search for one, but your efforts will be rewarded.

Pour your favorite white or light red wine with the meal.

Light Thanksgiving Dinner

✳

New Potato and Roast Red Pepper Salad

Roast Chicken with Parsley-Lemon Stuffing and Gravy

Minted Cranberry Sauce (recipe on page 16)

Parsley Biscuits

Creamed Onions

Broccoli with Sliced Almonds

Poached Winter Fruit with Lemon Whipped Cream

Serves 6–8

New Potato and Roast Red Pepper Salad

1 lb (500 g) red bell peppers (capsicums)
1½ lb (750 g) small red new potatoes
1 tablespoon plus ½ teaspoon salt
1 tablespoon fresh lemon juice
½ cup (4 fl oz/125 ml) olive oil
2 tablespoons chopped green (spring) onion
freshly ground pepper
1–2 bunches chicory (curly endive) or frisée, leaves separated and chilled

If you can find them, canned whole Spanish Lodosa red peppers are excellent for this, in which case use 4 or 5 canned peppers and omit the step of roasting and peeling. Some specialty-food stores carry them. All of the preparation up to assembly can be done in advance.

✳

Roast the bell peppers as directed in the glossary, page 104. Pull off the loosened skin and remove the core, seeds and ribs. Slice the peppers into long, thin strips and set aside.

Meanwhile, place the potatoes in a saucepan with water to cover and the 1 tablespoon salt. Bring to a boil, reduce the heat slightly, cover partially and cook gently until just tender, 25–30 minutes. Drain and set aside to cool.

In a small bowl stir together the lemon juice and the remaining ½ teaspoon salt until the salt dissolves. Add the olive oil, green onion and pepper to taste and whisk together until well mixed.

To serve, divide the chicory or frisée among 6–8 salad plates or place in a bowl. Cut the potatoes into thick slices and arrange atop the lettuce. Top with the red pepper strips. Whisk the dressing again, drizzle over the salad and serve.

Serves 6–8

Roast Chicken with Parsley-Lemon Stuffing

Serve with minted cranberry sauce (recipe on page 16).

✳

1 small loaf French bread, about 1 lb (500 g), preferably coarse sourdough

1 roasting chicken, 7–8 lb (3.5–4 kg), at room temperature

⅓ cup (½ oz/15 g) finely chopped fresh parsley

1 teaspoon crushed dried lemon thyme or regular thyme

finely grated zest of 1 lemon

2 eggs

3 tablespoons fresh lemon juice

½ cup (4 oz/125 g) unsalted butter, softened

salt and freshly ground pepper

Preheat an oven to 150°F (65°C). Cut the bread into thick slices; discard crusts. Tear into pieces and place in a food processor fitted with the metal blade. Process to form coarse crumbs. (You should have 5–6 cups.) Spread the crumbs on baking sheets and dry fully in the oven, 1½–2 hours; do not allow to color. Let cool.

Raise the heat to 325°F (165°C). Position a rack in the bottom third of the oven. Oil a V-shaped rack in a roasting pan. Rinse the chicken in cold water and dry with paper towels. Trim off all fat.

In a large bowl toss together the bread crumbs, parsley, thyme and lemon zest. In a small bowl lightly beat the eggs. Add the lemon juice, ¼ cup (2 oz/60 g) of the softened butter, 1 teaspoon salt and a little pepper. Mix well. Add the egg-butter mixture to the crumbs; toss to mix. Spoon loosely into the chicken cavity. Close with poultry pins and then truss (see page 9). Brush with some of the remaining butter. Sprinkle with salt and pepper and lay the bird on its side on the rack. Butter the shiny side of a piece of aluminum foil and lay, buttered side down, over the chicken.

Roast for 50 minutes. Turn onto its other side, brush with more butter, replace the foil and roast for another 50 minutes. Remove and save the foil. Turn breast-side up; brush with the remaining butter. Roast until golden brown, 20–30 minutes more. Test for doneness by inserting an instant-read thermometer in the thickest part of the thigh away from the bone; it should register 180°F (82°C).

Transfer to a warmed platter; cover loosely with the foil for about 10 minutes. Use the pan juices to make gravy (see page 14). Carve the chicken (see page 11) and serve with the stuffing and gravy.

Serves 6–8

Parsley Biscuits

2 cups (10 oz/315 g) all-purpose (plain) flour

½ teaspoon salt

1 tablespoon baking powder

finely shredded zest of 1 lemon

3 tablespoons finely chopped fresh parsley

½ cup (4 oz/125 g) vegetable shortening

½ cup (4 fl oz/125 ml) milk

¼ cup (2 fl oz/60 ml) heavy (double) cream

American biscuits are an excellent accompaniment to a holiday chicken or turkey dinner, and they are easy to prepare. Just have your ingredients measured and pans ready before you begin to mix the dough. Biscuits baked on baking sheets have more richly browned sides. Leftover biscuits can be placed in a plastic bag and refrigerated for up to 2 days; reheat in a 250°F (120°C) oven. These are delicious served with butter and minted cranberry sauce (recipe on page 16).

✳

Preheat an oven to 425°F (220°C). Grease 1 or 2 baking sheets or pans and set aside.

In a bowl stir together the flour, salt, baking powder, lemon zest and parsley. Add the shortening and, using a pastry blender, fingertips or 2 knives, mix together until the mixture resembles oatmeal. Add the milk and cream and, using a fork, mix together until the mixture forms a mass and holds together.

Gather up the dough into a ball, place on a floured board and knead a few times. Flatten the dough with your hands (or roll it out with a rolling pin) until it is ⅜–½ inch (9–12 mm) thick. Using a round cutter or glass 2–2½ inches (5–6 cm) in diameter, cut out as many biscuits as possible. Place on the prepared pan(s) about ¼ inch (6 mm) apart. Gather up scraps of dough and press together to make more biscuits.

Place in the oven and bake until golden and light, about 15 minutes. Serve hot.

Makes 20–24 biscuits

Creamed Onions

2 lb (1 kg) small white boiling onions, about 1½ inches (4 cm) in diameter, unpeeled

1 tablespoon plus ½ teaspoon salt

5 or 6 whole cloves

2 tablespoons unsalted butter

3 tablespoons all-purpose (plain) flour

2 cups (16 fl oz/500 ml) milk, heated

½ cup (4 fl oz/125 ml) heavy (double) cream, or as needed

3–4 tablespoons dry sherry

freshly ground pepper

3 tablespoons chopped fresh parsley

Small creamed onions have traditionally been a part of the Thanksgiving dinner. The onions can be prepared several hours ahead up to the point where they are added to the cream sauce, leaving only the making of sauce and assembly before serving. If small red boiling onions are available, use half white and half red onions.

✳

*F*ill a saucepan three-fourths full with water and bring to a boil. Add the onions and bring back to a boil. Cover partially and cook for 2–3 minutes; drain, then plunge into cold water to cool. Cut off the root ends; trim the stem ends if you like. Slip off the skins, then cut a shallow cross in the root end. (The cross keeps the inner onion segments from protruding out the onion top during cooking.) Return the onions to the saucepan and add water just to cover. Add the 1 tablespoon salt and the cloves and bring to a boil. Reduce the heat to low, cover partially and cook gently until just tender, 10–15 minutes. Drain, discarding the cloves, and set aside.

In the same saucepan over medium heat, melt the butter. Using a whisk stir in the flour. When it bubbles, cook, while stirring, for 1 minute. Slowly add the hot milk while whisking constantly. Continue whisking rapidly until smooth and thickened, 2–3 minutes. Whisk in the cream, sherry, the remaining ½ teaspoon salt and a little pepper. Taste for seasoning. If the sauce is too thick, add more cream to correct the consistency.

Add the prepared onions and reheat to just under a boil. Transfer to a serving dish, sprinkle with the parsley and serve at once.

Serves 6–8

Broccoli with Sliced Almonds

2–3 lb (1–1.5 kg) broccoli, depending
    upon the number of people being
    served
ice water
⅓ cup (1½ oz/45 g) sliced almonds
¼ cup (2 oz/60 g) unsalted butter
2 tablespoons salt
freshly grated nutmeg

Broccoli is always a good accompaniment to poultry. If the stems are thick, you will need to peel them so they will be tender enough to cook along with the florets. Be sure to crisp the broccoli in ice water before cooking. The ice water step is important because broccoli loses moisture after it is picked and the cold bath ensures it remains crisp during cooking.

✳

Using a sharp paring knife, cut off the broccoli florets from the stems. Peel the thickest stems, removing all of the tough, stringy outer surface. Cut into pieces ½–1 inch (12 mm–2.5 cm) long, depending upon the thickness of the stem. Place in a bowl with the florets and add ice water to cover. Set aside for 30 minutes.

Preheat an oven to 300°F (150°C). Spread the almonds on a baking sheet and toast in the oven until just beginning to show color, 5–6 minutes. Let cool.

Melt the butter in a small saucepan and set aside.

Fill a large pot three-fourths full with water, bring to a rapid boil and add the salt. Drain the broccoli well and plunge it into the boiling water. Bring back to a boil and cook, uncovered, until just tender yet still bright green and crisp, 3–5 minutes. Drain well.

Transfer the broccoli to a serving dish. Add the toasted almonds and a little nutmeg to the melted butter. Spoon over the broccoli and serve.

Serves 6–8

Poached Winter Fruit

3 cups (1½ lb/750 g) sugar
4½ cups (36 fl oz/1.1 l) water
2 lemons
4–6 ripe but firm pears
2 cups (8 oz/250 g) fresh cranberries
poached orange slices made from
   1 orange (*recipe on page 17*)
fresh mint sprigs for garnish
lemon whipped cream (*recipe on page 18*)

This simple dessert can be prepared a day ahead of time with only a few minutes required to assemble it just before serving. If you pierce the cranberries with a sharp toothpick, most of them will not burst during cooking. It is an added touch of perfection. Comice pears are particularly good for poaching because of both their flavor and texture.

✳

In a large sauté pan over medium heat, combine 2 cups (1 lb/ 500 g) of the sugar and 4 cups (32 fl oz/1 l) of the water. Bring to a boil, stirring to dissolve the sugar. Stir in the juice of 1 of the lemons. Keep warm.

In a large bowl put the juice of the remaining lemon. Peel, halve and core the pears. Immediately place each pear half in the bowl, turning it in the juice to coat. When all the halves are coated, transfer them to the hot syrup along with any lemon juice left in the bowl. Bring to a simmer and cook gently, uncovered, turning each half a couple of times to poach evenly, until tender, 10–15 minutes. Let the pears cool in their poaching liquid.

In a separate saucepan combine the remaining 1 cup (½ lb/250 g) sugar and the remaining ½ cup (4 fl oz/125 ml) water. Bring to a boil, stirring constantly. Reduce the heat to low and add the cranberries. Simmer gently, stirring a couple times, until the cranberries are just tender and the syrup thickens, 4–5 minutes; do not overcook. Let cool.

To serve, use a slotted spoon to transfer the pears, core side up, to a deep serving platter or serving dish. Add about one-third of their syrup to the dish. Using the same spoon to drain off some of their syrup, arrange cranberries over each pear half. Then, using tongs, place the orange slices over and in between the pears. Garnish with the mint. Serve the lemon whipped cream in a bowl on the side.

Serves 6–8

In the busy and mobile age in which we live, the holiday table sometimes seems to be shrinking: Rather than a gathering of the generations, as often as not we welcome just a few close relatives or friends for Thanksgiving. That fact inspired me to create a menu that, although no less festive or generous, does not aim for the grand scale of old-fashioned feasts.

Key to the menu's success is how easy it is now to buy a fresh bone-in turkey breast from well-stocked food stores or butcher shops. It is easier and faster to roast than a whole turkey, and serves six to eight people with minimal leftovers. And most people prefer the breast meat anyway.

As simple as this menu is, good organization will make it even easier. There are a number of things you can do the day before: cooking and puréeing the carrots for the soup; preparing and drying the bread crumbs for the dressing; making the cranberry sauce; cooking the lentils; and assembling all the other ingredients. The pumpkin cheesecake actually *must* be made a day in advance, for the best texture and flavor.

If you don't have a double oven, just bake the turkey breast, dressing and onions in the same oven.

Offer your favorite white or light red wine with this menu.

Cozy Thanksgiving Dinner

✷

Carrot and Mint Soup

Roast Whole Turkey Breast with Fennel
and Bay Leaves and Gravy

Baked Pork and Grape Dressing

Apple-Orange Cranberry Sauce
(recipe on page 17)

Baked Onions with Tomato Sauce

Braised Cabbage and Lentils

Pumpkin Cheesecake

Serves 6–8

Carrot and Mint Soup

2 tablespoons unsalted butter

2 yellow onions, diced (about 1½ cups/ 8 oz/250 g)

10–12 carrots, peeled and sliced (about 4 cups/1 lb/500 g)

4 cups (32 fl oz/1 l) chicken stock, preferably homemade (recipe on page 13)

3 large fresh mint sprigs

2 cups (16 fl oz/500 ml) milk

1 cup (8 fl oz/250 ml) heavy (double) cream

salt

paprika

sour cream

chopped fresh mint

This soup can be made up to 24 hours in advance, through the step of puréeing the vegetables; combine the purée and cooking liquid, then cover and refrigerate. Fresh mint is preferred, but if it is unavailable, substitute 2 teaspoons crushed dried mint, adding it with the carrots; omit the chopped mint garnish. The leftover soup can be stored in a covered bowl in the refrigerator for 1 day, then reheated slowly to serve.

✫

*I*n a large saucepan over medium heat, melt the butter. Add the onion and sauté until translucent, 2–3 minutes. Add the carrots, stock and mint sprigs. Cover and simmer over low heat until the carrots are tender, 25–30 minutes. Remove the mint sprigs and discard.

Place a colander over a bowl and pour the contents of the pan into the colander. Reserve the cooking liquid. Put the vegetables in a food processor fitted with the metal blade and purée until smooth. Return the purée and the reserved liquid to the saucepan. Over medium-low heat, stir in the milk and cream. Season to taste with salt and a little paprika and heat almost to a boil; do not allow the soup to boil.

Serve with a dollop of sour cream and a sprinkling of chopped mint on each serving.

Serves 6–8 with leftovers

Roast Whole Turkey Breast with Fennel and Bay Leaves

6–7 lb (3–3.5 kg) whole turkey breast with breastbone in, at room temperature

1 yellow onion, cut into large cubes

1 lemon, cut into quarters

2 or 3 bay leaves

1 small fennel bulb, preferably with stalks intact, sliced

salt and freshly ground pepper

¼ cup (2 oz/60 g) unsalted butter, melted

Seek out a market that sells fresh turkeys. Be sure the neck and back bones have been removed, so the breast lays flat, and remember to remove the breast from the refrigerator about 45 minutes before roasting. If you can find dried fennel stalks, use 3 or 4 pieces, each about 6 inches (15 cm) long, instead of the fresh. Pass apple-orange cranberry sauce (recipe on page 17) at the table.

✦

Preheat an oven to 350°F (180°C). Position a rack in the bottom third of the oven. Lightly oil a flat rack in a roasting pan.

Rinse the turkey breast in cold water and pat dry with paper towels. Place skin-side down on a flat surface. Place the onion, lemon, bay leaves and fennel in the breast cavity. Sprinkle with salt and pepper. Place the oiled rack, upside down, over the turkey cavity and, holding the rack tightly against the cavity, turn the breast over and place in the roasting pan, skin-side up. Brush with some of the melted butter and cover loosely with aluminum foil.

Roast for 50 minutes, basting a couple of times with the butter. Remove the foil and reserve it. Continue to roast, basting several times with the pan juices, until the breast is golden and cooked through, 50–60 minutes longer. Test for doneness by inserting an instant-read thermometer in the thickest part of the breast away from bone. It should register 165°–170°F (74°–77°C), but not more than 170°F or the meat will be dry.

Transfer the breast to a warmed platter and cover loosely with the foil until ready to carve, about 20 minutes. Meanwhile, use the pan juices to make the gravy (recipe on page 14).

Carve the turkey breast (see page 10) and serve with the gravy.

Serves 6–8

Baked Pork and Grape Dressing

1 loaf French bread, about 1 lb (500 g)

2 tablespoons unsalted butter, or as needed

1 lb (500 g) ground (minced) pork

2 teaspoons crushed dried sage leaves

1 teaspoon salt

¼ teaspoon freshly ground black pepper

pinch of cayenne pepper

½ cup (3 oz/90 g) diced yellow onion

½ cup (3 oz/90 g) diced celery

1 small tart apple, peeled, cored and chopped

1 cup (6 oz/185 g) seedless green grapes, stemmed

½ cup (4 fl oz/125 ml) chicken stock, preferably homemade (*recipe on page 13*)

3 eggs, lightly beaten

This dressing is a nice accompaniment to roast turkey and gravy. Prepare the bread crumbs well ahead of time so they dry properly.

✶

Preheat an oven to 150°F (65°C). Slice or tear the bread, including the crusts, into small pieces. Place in a food processor fitted with the metal blade and process to form coarse crumbs. (You should have 8–9 cups.) Spread the crumbs on baking sheets and dry fully in the oven, about 2 hours. The crumbs should not color. Let cool.

Raise the oven temperature to 350°F (180°C). Butter a 2- or 2½-qt (2- or 2.5-l) baking dish.

In a large frying pan over medium heat, melt the 2 tablespoons butter. Add the pork and stir, breaking it up with a fork until crumbly, about 8 minutes (cook the pork in two batches if the pan is not big enough to spread out the meat). Add the sage, salt, black pepper and cayenne and continue stirring and tossing until lightly browned, 4–5 minutes longer. Using a slotted spoon transfer the meat to a plate, leaving the drippings in the pan.

Add the onion and celery to the pan, adding butter if needed, and sauté until translucent, 1–2 minutes. Add the chopped apple and grapes and stir and toss over medium heat for 2 minutes. Set aside.

Put the bread crumbs into a large bowl. In a separate bowl stir together the chicken stock and eggs. While rapidly tossing the crumbs, gradually add the stock-egg mixture; the crumbs should be evenly moistened.

Mix in the reserved meat and the apple-grape mixture. Taste and adjust the seasoning. Spoon loosely into the prepared baking dish. Place in the oven and bake until golden, 40–50 minutes.

Serves 6–8

Baked Onions with Tomato Sauce

6–8 yellow onions
6–8 plum (Roma) tomatoes
1 teaspoon crushed dried oregano
salt and freshly ground pepper
2–3 tablespoons extra-virgin olive oil

Here is a dish that is best served the moment it comes out of the oven. The onions and tomatoes can be prepared and assembled in a baking dish several hours before baking. Use a good-quality extra-virgin olive oil. If fresh, flavorful plum tomatoes are unavailable, use canned whole plum tomatoes with some of their liquid.

✯

Preheat an oven to 350°F (180°C). Position a rack in the middle of the oven. Select a baking dish large enough to hold the whole onions in a single layer and brush the bottom and sides with olive oil.

Peel each onion and cut a shallow cross in the root end. (The cross keeps the inner onion segments from protruding out the top during baking.) Place in the baking dish, root end down.

Fill a saucepan three-fourths full with water and bring to a boil. Core each tomato and cut a shallow cross in the base. Plunge the tomatoes into the boiling water and leave for 1 minute. Using a slotted spoon, remove the tomatoes. When cool enough to handle, peel off the skins. Cut the tomatoes in half crosswise and squeeze out the seeds. Chop coarsely and arrange around the onions.

Sprinkle the onions and tomatoes with the oregano and salt and pepper to taste. Drizzle with the olive oil. Cover the dish loosely with aluminum foil. Bake until the onions are tender, 45–50 minutes.

Transfer the onions to a serving dish and top each onion with some of the tomato sauce.

Serves 6–8

Braised Cabbage and Lentils

1 cup (7 oz/220 g) lentils
4 cups (32 fl oz/1 l) water
1½ teaspoons salt
1 green cabbage, about 1½ lb (750 g)
¼ cup (2 oz/60 g) unsalted butter
½ cup (4 fl oz/125 ml) dry white wine
1 tablespoon fresh lemon juice
freshly grated nutmeg

A good winter vegetable combination. The lentils can be cooked a day in advance and even the cabbage can be shredded several hours ahead of time. That leaves only the final assembly, which must be done about half an hour before serving and is quite easy. Do not overcook the lentils; they should be tender but remain whole.

★

Combine the lentils, water and 1 teaspoon of the salt in a saucepan over medium heat. Bring just to a simmer, then adjust the heat so the lentils barely simmer, cover partially and cook until just tender, 25–30 minutes. Drain well; set aside.

Cut the cabbage in half and then slice lengthwise into thin shreds or slice on a mandoline. In a large sauté pan or frying pan over medium heat, melt the butter. Add the cabbage, cover and let steam over very low heat, stirring several times, 8–10 minutes.

Stir in the lentils, the remaining ½ teaspoon salt and the wine. Cover partially and cook gently, stirring occasionally, until the cabbage is just tender, about 15 minutes.

Stir in the lemon juice and a little nutmeg. Taste and adjust the seasoning. Transfer to a serving dish and serve immediately.

Serves 6–8

Pumpkin Cheesecake

1½ cups (5 oz/155 g) graham cracker crumbs

3 tablespoons plus 1 cup (8 oz/250 g) sugar

1 teaspoon ground ginger

6 tablespoons (3 oz/90 g) unsalted butter, melted

1½ lb (750 g) cream cheese, at room temperature

1¾ cups (1 lb/500 g) pumpkin purée, at room temperature

1 teaspoon finely grated orange zest

1 tablespoon ground cinnamon

½ teaspoon ground cloves

½ teaspoon ground nutmeg

6 eggs, lightly beaten

Make this cheesecake the day before serving. The cream cheese, pumpkin purée and eggs must be at room temperature before mixing. Covering the outside of the pan with aluminum foil helps the cheesecake to cook slowly and evenly. Use confectioners' (icing) sugar to stencil leaf or other designs on top, if you like. Slice the cheesecake while it is still well chilled.

✫

Preheat an oven to 325°F (165°C). Position a rack in the middle of the oven. Cover the outside (bottom and sides) of a 9-inch (23-cm) springform pan with heavy-duty aluminum foil, shiny side out. Butter the inside of the pan and set aside.

In a bowl stir together the cracker crumbs, the 3 tablespoons sugar and the ginger. Stir and toss while gradually adding the melted butter. Continue to stir and toss until well mixed. Press the crumb mixture evenly over the inside of the pan to reach 1¾–2 inches (about 5 cm) up the sides. Chill for 30 minutes.

Place the cream cheese in a large bowl. Using an electric mixer set on medium speed, beat until light and fluffy, 2–3 minutes. Slowly add the 1 cup (8 oz/250 g) sugar while continuously beating; occasionally scrape down the bowl sides. Add the pumpkin, orange zest, cinnamon, cloves and nutmeg and beat until smooth. Add the eggs, a little at a time, beating well after each addition and scraping down the bowl sides. Using a rubber spatula stir slowly to dispel some of the bubbles.

Pour the batter in the prepared pan and smooth the surface. Bake until the top is lightly puffed all over, 60–70 minutes. The center may be slightly underset; it will firm up during cooling. Cool on a wire rack, then remove the foil and pan sides and refrigerate overnight. Before serving, you may want to carefully slip the chilled cake onto a large, flat serving plate if you have one.

Serves 6–8 with leftovers

Roast prime rib of beef stars in this menu, as it has for centuries on English holiday tables. Popovers, a variation on the traditional accompaniment of Yorkshire pudding, and horseradish sauce brightened by cranberries help to round out a robust table.

Serving the beef at its best requires a little special attention. First, seek out the highest-quality well-aged roast you can afford, purchased from a good butcher shop. Carefully read through all the recipes in the menu, then organize the meal's preparation so that nothing distracts you from roasting the beef to the desired degree of doneness ready to serve at the appointed time.

The day before the dinner, make the cranberry horseradish sauce. Trim and wash the Swiss chard, then refrigerate in a plastic bag to crisp overnight. The salad, vegetables and popover ingredients can be at least partially assembled up to several hours ahead.

Be sure to remove the beef from the refrigerator 2–2½ hours before you begin to cook it. Start making the steamed pudding after the meat goes into the oven.

To complement the roast beef, pour a medium- to full-bodied red wine.

Festive Christmas Dinner

✦

Waldorf Salad with Mustard Dressing

Roast Prime Rib of Beef

Cranberry Horseradish Sauce
(recipe on page 16)

Popovers

Glazed Carrots and Parsnips

Swiss Chard with Ham

Cranberry-Orange Steamed Pudding with
Brandy Butter Sauce

Serves 8–10

Waldorf Salad with Mustard Dressing

¾ cup (3 oz/90 g) walnut or pecan
   halves
4 crisp, firm apples, such as pippin,
   McIntosh or Rome
juice of 1 lemon
1 cup (5 oz/155 g) finely diced celery
½ cup (3 oz/90 g) diced red bell pepper
   (capsicum)
3 green (spring) onions, including part of
   tender green tops, finely chopped
¾ cup (6 fl oz/180 ml) sour cream
1 tablespoon Dijon mustard
1½ tablespoons honey
1 teaspoon minced fresh mint
salt and freshly ground pepper
1–2 heads Bibb lettuce

Classic Waldorf salad, created at the original Waldorf Astoria Hotel in New York, consists of red apples, celery, walnuts and mayonnaise. Sometimes grapes are included. This version adds onion, bell pepper and a mustard–sour cream dressing. The salad may be assembled, except for the dressing, about 2 hours before the meal, covered and stored in the refrigerator. Add the dressing just before serving.

✧

*P*reheat an oven to 200°F (95°C). Spread the nut halves on a baking sheet and lightly toast in the oven, 6–7 minutes; they should not brown. Chop coarsely and set aside.

Peel, quarter and core the apples. Cut into about ½-inch (12-mm) dice and toss with the lemon juice in a bowl. Add the celery, bell pepper, green onions and nuts.

In a separate bowl combine the sour cream, mustard, honey and mint. Whisk together until well blended. Season to taste with salt and pepper. (More mustard, honey or mint may be added, if desired.)

Separate the lettuce leaves and use only the crisp inner leaves; reserve the larger leaves for another use. Arrange around the rim of a serving plate. Add the dressing to the apple mixture and mix well. Spoon into the center of the plate.

Serves 8–10

Roast Prime Rib of Beef

prime rib roast with 3–4 bones, 7–8 lb (3.5–4 kg) trimmed weight, at room temperature

salt and freshly ground pepper, optional

½ cup (4 fl oz/125 ml) water, or as needed

A prime rib roast is an excellent choice for Christmas dinner. The beef must be chosen with care, however, for its flavor is of utmost importance. Seek out a butcher who carries high-quality dry-aged beef. The roast will cost a little more, but this special occasion merits it. Ask the butcher to tie the roast. Sprinkling the outside of a roast with salt, pepper or herbs has little effect on the flavor of the meat inside, although it does add taste and texture to the surface of the roast. Remove the meat from the refrigerator 2–2½ hours before cooking, to bring it to room temperature. Serve with cranberry horseradish sauce (recipe on page 16).

✦

Preheat an oven to 500°F (260°C). Position a rack in the bottom third of the oven.

In a roasting pan without a rack, place the roast rib-side down (fat-side up). Sprinkle with pepper, if desired. If you wish to salt the roast, do so toward the end of roasting. Roast for 15 minutes. Reduce the heat to 325°F (165°C) and continue roasting.

After 1½ hours of roasting, start testing for doneness by inserting an instant-read thermometer in the thickest part of the meat away from the bone; it should register 130°F (55°C) for medium-rare. It should reach this point 2–2½ hours after you turned down the heat. See page 9 for temperatures for other degrees of doneness.

Transfer the roast to a warmed platter. Cover loosely with aluminum foil and let rest until ready to carve, 15–20 minutes. Meanwhile, pour off just the fat from the pan and heat the remaining juices over medium heat. Add the water and deglaze the pan by stirring to dislodge any browned bits stuck to the pan. Bring to a boil and season to taste with salt and pepper. Add more water for desired consistency and taste.

Carve the beef (see page 12) and serve with the pan juices in a bowl on the side.

Serves 8–10

Popovers

2 eggs
¼ teaspoon salt
1 cup (8 fl oz/250 ml) milk
2 tablespoons unsalted butter, melted
1 cup (5 oz/155 g) all-purpose (plain)
  flour

Have the ingredients measured and ready for quick assembly, as the popovers need to be baked just before serving time. Popovers can be baked in muffin tins as well as popover pans. The muffin size is particularly nice for a holiday dinner. Traditionally popovers are slipped into a hot oven and the heat immediately makes the moist batter rise into a light bread. According to famed cookbook author Marion Cunningham, the best way to bake popovers is to start them in a cold oven. I have tried this method and it works beautifully, although you will need a double oven. Or, lacking two ovens, bake them after the beef is removed: increase the temperature to 425°F (220°C) and bake as directed below; they may not take as long.

✧

*B*utter 12 standard-size muffin-tin cups or a popover pan.

In a bowl combine the eggs and salt. Using a whisk beat lightly. Stir in the milk and butter and then beat in the flour just until blended. Do not overbeat.

Fill each cup about half full and place in a cold oven. Set the oven temperature to 425°F (220°C) and bake for 20 minutes. Reduce the heat to 375°F (190°C) and bake until the popovers are golden, 10–15 minutes longer. They should be crisp on the outside.

Quickly pierce each popover with a thin metal skewer or the tip of a small knife to release the steam. Leave in the oven a couple of minutes for further crisping, then remove and serve at once.

Makes 12 popovers

Glazed Carrots and Parsnips

1½ lb (750 g) carrots
1 lb (500 g) parsnips
1 cup (8 fl oz/250 ml) water
½ teaspoon salt
4 tablespoons (2 oz/60 g) unsalted butter
½ cup (3 oz/90 g) firmly packed brown
   sugar
3 tablespoons Madeira wine
½ teaspoon finely grated fresh ginger
fresh mint, parsley or sage, chopped or
   whole sprigs, for garnish

These two vegetables complement each other nicely. They can be prepared in advance up to the point of glazing. Additional carrots may be substituted for the parsnips.

✧

*P*eel the carrots and parsnips. Cut into 3-inch (7.5-cm) lengths. Slice each piece in half lengthwise and slice the thick upper portions into quarters lengthwise, so the pieces are of equal size for cooking. Put them into a saucepan with the water, salt and 2 tablespoons of the butter. Cover tightly and simmer very gently over low heat until just tender, 10–15 minutes. Drain and set aside.

In a sauté pan or frying pan over medium heat, melt the remaining 2 tablespoons butter. Add the sugar, wine and ginger. Cook while stirring, until the sugar dissolves. Reduce the heat and continue to cook until reduced and thickened, 2–3 minutes. Add the carrots and parsnips and toss until well coated. Cook until the vegetables are heated through, 2–3 minutes.

Transfer to a serving dish; garnish with mint, parsley or sage.

Serves 8–10

Swiss Chard with Ham

4–5 lb (2–2.5 kg) red or green Swiss chard
2 tablespoons unsalted butter
1 yellow onion, diced
¾–1 lb (375–500 g) cooked ham,
   trimmed of fat and cut into short strips
salt and freshly ground pepper
2 lemons

Swiss chard is one vegetable that deserves more attention from cooks. It is easy to prepare and goes well with most roasts. Select young, tender leaves if possible. Purchase a slice of freshly cut ham about ⅜ inch (9 mm) thick from a good meat market or from a butcher in the meat department of a quality supermarket.

✧

Cut off the tough stems from the Swiss chard leaves, including 1–2 inches (2.5–5 cm) into the leaves; discard the stems. Wash the leaves well, drain and shake off excess water. Pile the leaves flat and slice into strips 1 inch (2.5 cm) wide. Set aside.

In a large sauté pan or saucepan over medium heat, melt the butter. Add the onion and cook gently until translucent, 3–4 minutes. Add the ham and cook for another 3–4 minutes, stirring frequently. Add the Swiss chard, reduce the heat, cover and cook for about 10 minutes. Remove the cover, stir and check for doneness by tasting a piece of ham; it should be tender to the bite. If more cooking is needed or too much liquid has collected, raise the heat and cook, uncovered, for 1–2 minutes.

Season to taste with salt and pepper. Using 1 of the lemons, squeeze in juice to taste. Transfer to a serving dish. Cut the remaining lemon into wedges for garnish.

Serves 8–10

Cranberry-Orange Steamed Pudding

½ cup (4 fl oz/125 ml) cold water

1⅓ cups (11 oz/340 g) sugar

1 cup (4 oz/125 g) dried cranberries

2½ cups (12½ oz/390 g) all-purpose (plain) flour

1½ teaspoons baking soda (bicarbonate of soda)

¼ teaspoon ground cloves

⅛ teaspoon ground allspice

⅛ teaspoon ground ginger

½ cup (4 oz/125 g) unsalted butter, at room temperature

3 eggs, lightly beaten

½ cup (4 fl oz/125 ml) freshly squeezed orange juice

⅓ cup (2 oz/60 g) crystallized ginger, chopped

1 tablespoon finely grated orange zest

boiling water, as needed

brandy butter sauce *(recipe on page 19)*

If you do not have a steamed pudding mold, which has a "clamp-on" cover and sometimes a central tube, use any deep mold or small ovenproof mixing bowl. Just cover with a piece of buttered aluminum foil (buttered side in) and fasten securely with kitchen string.

✧

*B*utter the inside of a 1½–2 qt (48–64 fl oz/1.5–2 l) pudding mold and its cover. Select a pot (with a cover) large enough to hold the mold. Place a low trivet or jar lid in the pot bottom.

In a small pan combine the cold water with ⅓ cup (3 oz/90 g) of the sugar. Bring to a boil, stirring to dissolve the sugar. Add the cranberries, cover and simmer for 2–3 minutes. Set aside.

In a bowl stir together the flour, baking soda, cloves, allspice and ground ginger. Set aside. In a large bowl combine the butter and the remaining 1 cup (8 oz/250 g) sugar. Using an electric mixer set at medium speed, beat until light and fluffy, about 3 minutes, scraping down the bowl sides as needed. Add the eggs, a little at a time, beating after each addition. Beat until increased in volume slightly, 5–6 minutes, again scraping down the bowl sides.

Using a rubber spatula fold in the flour mixture, one third at a time, alternating it with the orange juice and the cranberries and their liquid. Quickly beat in the crystallized ginger and zest. Spoon into the prepared mold, avoiding air bubbles. Cover the mold and place on the trivet in the pot. Add boiling water to reach two-thirds up the mold sides. Cover the pot and simmer gently for 1½ hours. Add boiling water as needed to maintain original level.

Remove the mold and let rest for 5 minutes. Invert onto a serving plate and lift off the mold. While still warm, cut into wedges and serve with brandy butter sauce.

Serves 8–10

If you want to host a Christmas dinner that allows a more relaxed pace, a baked ham is an excellent choice for the main course. It requires little preparation, is easy to bake and keeps well. I've filled out the menu with other dishes that match the ham's casual, homey style, including corn bread, a sweet potato pudding, fresh peas and a pie filled with apples and cranberries.

In the spirit of the main course, all the accompanying recipes are prepared at least partly in advance, leaving you very little that needs to be done at the last minute.

The day before, you could trim the ham, if necessary, and poach the orange slices to go with it; wash and refrigerate the salad greens; shell the peas; cook and purée the sweet potatoes; and assemble all the other ingredients. The pie may be made the morning of the dinner.

And don't worry if you do not have a double oven: The ham and pudding can bake in the same oven, and bake the corn bread ahead of time, reheating it just before serving, if you like.

A light red wine will go nicely with the ham.

Casual Christmas Dinner

❖

Pear, Walnut and Goat Cheese Salad with Honey Dressing

Glazed Ham with Poached Orange Slices

Whole Kernel Corn Bread

Fresh Peas and Water Chestnuts

Sweet Potato-Ginger Pudding

Gingered Apple-Cranberry Pie with Lemon Whipped Cream

Serves 8–10

Pear, Walnut and Goat Cheese Salad

3–4 large bunches watercress

4 or 5 ripe but firm pears

2 or 3 lemons

½ teaspoon salt

3 tablespoons honey, preferably thyme honey

½ cup (4 fl oz/125 ml) mild extra-virgin olive oil

freshly ground pepper

1½ cups (6 oz/185 g) walnut halves, broken into small pieces

½ lb (250 g) feta cheese, crumbled

I prefer Comice pears for this salad, but Anjou or Bartlett are good too. Be sure the pears are ripe but still firm. A good, natural goat's or sheep's milk feta cheese has the best flavor and crumbles well for a salad.

✤

Wash and trim the watercress, removing and discarding the tough stems and old leaves. Drain, dry and wrap in a clean, damp kitchen towel. Place in the refrigerator for at least 1 hour to chill and crisp.

Peel, quarter and core the pears. Cut each quarter into 3 lengthwise slices and place in a bowl with the juice of 1 lemon. Toss carefully and thoroughly to keep the flesh from turning brown.

Squeeze 3 tablespoons of juice from 1 or 2 lemons into a small bowl. Add the salt and stir to dissolve. Whisk in the honey, and then the olive oil and a little pepper. Taste and adjust the seasoning.

Arrange the watercress on individual salad plates and top with the pear slices. Scatter the walnut pieces and crumbled cheese over the top. Whisk the dressing again and drizzle over the salad or pass it separately in a bowl.

Serves 8–10

Glazed Ham with Poached Orange Slices

10–12 lb (5–6 kg) bone-in ham, preferably one only partially cooked, at room temperature

2–3 cups (16–24 fl oz/500–750 ml) Madeira wine

¾ cup (6 oz/185 g) firmly packed brown sugar

poached orange slices made from 2 oranges (*recipe on page 17*)

A partially cooked ("cook before eating") ham from a specialty meat market or the meat department of a large, quality food market with butchers in attendance is the best choice. It is superior in flavor and texture to hams that are tenderized and fully baked. If a small whole ham is not available, ask for the butt end of a large ham; butchers in good markets will gladly cut the size you need. Remove the ham from the refrigerator 1½–2 hours before cooking, to bring it to room temperature.

❖

Preheat an oven to 350°F (180°C). Position a rack in the lower third of the oven.

Wipe the ham with a damp cloth. Trim off any skin and excess fat. Place on a flat rack in a roasting pan, fat-side down; put into the oven. Using a brush or kitchen spoon, baste frequently with some of the wine and bake for about 1½ hours, or until the internal temperature registers 130°F (55°C). To test, insert an instant-read thermometer in the thickest part of the ham away from the bone. Remove the ham from the oven and turn it fat-side up. In a small bowl stir together the sugar and enough wine to form a thick paste. Spread on top of the ham.

Return to the oven. Bake, continuing to baste 2 or 3 times with wine or with the pan juices if the wine is used up, until the internal temperature registers 160°F (70°C), another 30–45 minutes. The ham should be a rich burgundy color.

Transfer to a warmed platter, cover loosely with aluminum foil and let rest for at least 10–15 minutes before carving.

Garnish the ham with the orange slices and then carve (see page 11). Include an orange slice with each serving.

Serves 8–10

Whole Kernel Corn Bread

3 large ears yellow corn, husks and silks
  removed
1¼ cups (8 oz/250 g) yellow cornmeal,
  preferably stone-ground
¾ cup (4 oz/125 g) all-purpose (plain)
  flour
2 teaspoons sugar
1¼ teaspoons salt
1 tablespoon baking powder
⅛ teaspoon cayenne pepper
2 eggs, lightly beaten
1 cup (8 fl oz/250 ml) milk
¼ cup (2 oz/60 g) unsalted butter, melted

If a food shop in your area sells stone-ground cornmeal, buy it for this recipe. It makes a nicely textured, well-flavored bread. If there is any bread left over, slice it and toast it in the oven. It is excellent served for breakfast with almost any fruit jam. If you cannot find fresh corn, use frozen or canned whole kernel corn. If using frozen corn, cook it as directed in the recipe. Canned corn need only be well drained before adding to the batter.

❖

*P*reheat an oven to 425°F (220°C). Position a rack in the middle of the oven. Butter an 8–9-inch (20–23-cm) square baking pan that is 1½ inches (4 cm) deep.

Fill a large saucepan three-fourths full with water and bring to a boil. Add the corn and cook for 5 minutes. Drain and immediately plunge into cold water to cool. Using a sharp knife and holding each ear of corn upright on a cutting surface, cut the kernels from the cobs. You should have 1½–2 cups (9–12 oz/280–375 g) kernels. Set aside.

In a bowl stir together the cornmeal, flour, sugar, salt, baking powder and cayenne pepper. Stir in the eggs and milk, then the corn kernels and butter.

Pour the batter into the prepared pan. Bake until golden, 25–30 minutes.

Remove from the oven and let cool slightly on a rack for 2–3 minutes. Cut into squares and serve warm.

Serves 8–10

Fresh Peas and Water Chestnuts

3–4 lb (1.5–2 kg) peas in the shell
   (about 4 cups/1¼ lb/625 g shelled)
4 tablespoons (2 oz/60 g) unsalted butter
¼ cup (1½ oz/45 g) chopped yellow
   onion
1½ cups (8–10 oz/250–300 g) well-
   drained canned water chestnuts, thinly
   sliced
¼ cup (2 fl oz/60 ml) water
½ teaspoon salt, plus salt for seasoning
1 tablespoon finely minced fresh mint
¼ cup (2 fl oz/60 ml) heavy (double)
   cream

Fresh mint and a little cream bring these two diverse vegetables together in a pleasantly flavorful union. Finding fresh peas and shelling them is worth the effort. This step can be done 4–6 hours in advance, or even the day before the dinner.

❖

Shell the peas and refrigerate until needed.

In a saucepan over medium heat, melt 2 tablespoons of the butter. Add the onion and sauté gently until translucent, about 2 minutes. Add the water chestnuts and cook, stirring, about 2 minutes. Set aside.

In another saucepan combine the water, the remaining 2 tablespoons butter and the salt. Bring to a boil and add the peas. Cover and cook until just tender, 2–3 minutes.

Meanwhile, return the saucepan with the onions and water chestnuts to medium-low heat. Add the mint and cream and stir until heated through.

When the peas are tender, drain well and combine with the onions, water chestnuts and cream. Toss well. Season to taste with salt, transfer to a warmed serving dish and serve.

Serves 8–10

Sweet Potato–Ginger Pudding

2 lb (1 kg) yellow-fleshed sweet potatoes,
  unpeeled

finely grated zest of 1 lemon

½ teaspoon salt

⅓ cup (2 oz/60 g) crystallized ginger,
  finely chopped

1½ cups (12 fl oz/375 ml) heavy (double)
  cream

¼ teaspoon freshly grated nutmeg

4 egg whites

Here is an ideal vegetable accompaniment to baked ham or turkey. The sweet potatoes can be boiled and puréed in advance and all the ingredients assembled for the final mixing and baking. If yellow sweet potatoes are not available or you prefer the orange-fleshed ones (what Americans call yams), use them. Brush off any excess sugar from the crystallized ginger. If you do not have two ovens, bake the pudding in the same oven with the ham.

❖

Place the sweet potatoes in a large saucepan with water to cover. Bring to a boil, reduce the heat, cover and cook until tender, 30–40 minutes. Drain and let cool.

Meanwhile, preheat an oven to 350°F (180°C). Position a rack in the middle of the oven. Butter a 2-qt (2-l) soufflé dish or baking dish.

Peel the cooled sweet potatoes and place in a food processor fitted with the metal blade. Process to a smooth purée. You should have about 2½ cups (1¼ lb/625 g). Transfer the purée to a large bowl and stir in the lemon zest, salt and crystallized ginger. Then stir in the cream and add nutmeg to taste.

In a separate bowl, using an electric mixer set on medium speed, beat the egg whites until soft folds form. Add about one-fourth of the beaten whites to the potato mixture and stir in well to lighten it. Then, using a rubber spatula, gently fold in the remaining whites, being careful not to deflate the mixture. Spoon into the prepared baking dish.

Bake until risen and slightly golden on top, 40–50 minutes. Serve immediately.

Serves 8–10

Gingered Apple-Cranberry Pie

pastry for a 9-inch (23-cm) double-crust
  pie *(recipe on page 18)*
5 large, tart apples such as pippin, Granny
  Smith or McIntosh, peeled, cored and
  thinly sliced lengthwise
⅓ cup (2 oz/60 g) crystallized ginger,
  finely chopped
1 cup (4 oz/125 g) fresh cranberries,
  coarsely chopped
finely grated zest of 1 lemon
3 tablespoons all-purpose (plain) flour
1 cup (8 oz/250 g) granulated sugar
¼ teaspoon salt
¼ teaspoon ground allspice
3 tablespoons unsalted butter, cut into
  small bits
2–3 tablespoons heavy (double) cream
1–2 tablespoons demerara sugar or
  raw sugar
lemon whipped cream *(recipe on page 18)*

This pie tastes best when still slightly warm, but it can be baked 3 or 4 hours in advance and served at room temperature.

❖

Preheat an oven to 425°F (220°C).

On a lightly floured surface, roll out the larger pastry portion into an 11-inch (28-cm) round. Fit carefully into a 9-inch (23-cm) pie pan. Trim the pastry so there is about 1 inch (2.5 cm) overhang. Fold the overhang under and press it down against the pan rim. Roll out the remaining pastry into a 10-inch (25-cm) round for the top crust. Set the prepared pie pan and top crust aside.

In a large bowl combine the apples, ginger, cranberries and lemon zest. In a small bowl toss together the flour, granulated sugar, salt and allspice. Add to the bowl of fruit and toss well. Arrange the fruit in the prepared pan, piling it high in the center. Dot with the butter. Brush the pastry rim with water and lay the top crust over the fruit. Press down around the rim, then trim and flute or leave a plain edge. Make 2 or 3 slits in the top.

Press together the pastry scraps and roll out ⅛ inch (3 mm) thick. Cut out leaf and berry shapes and use to decorate the pie. Brush the top with cream where you wish to place decorations. Press the leaves and berries in place. Lightly brush the crust, including the decorations, with cream. Sprinkle with the demerara or raw sugar.

Bake for 15 minutes. Reduce the heat to 350°F (180°C) and continue baking until the crust is golden and the fruit is tender when pierced through one of the slits, 50–55 minutes longer.

Transfer to a rack to cool. Serve slightly warm or at room temperature. Accompany with the lemon whipped cream.

Serves 8–10

$\mathcal{A}$ roast leg of lamb makes an interesting change of pace from the usual Christmas main course, yet it is no less festive. Here, it becomes the centerpiece of a menu full of lively flavors that will excite favorable comments from friends who enjoy something a little bit out of the ordinary. Of course, you could also serve this menu at other times of the year—particularly at Easter, when lamb is a more traditional choice.

If you read through the recipes carefully and take a little time to organize yourself, the day of the party can be relaxing. Be sure to order your leg of lamb well ahead of time from a good butcher shop or food store, to ensure that you put the best-quality meat on your table.

Up to a day in advance, you can make the chutney and bread; cook and purée the squash for the soup; and wash the spinach, putting it in the refrigerator to crisp. The lamb, potatoes and pudding can all bake in the same oven, if necessary, or you can bake the pudding just before the lamb.

A medium-bodied red wine would go well with the roast lamb.

Christmas Dinner For Friends

*

Cream of Squash Soup

Roast Leg of Lamb

Apple-Mint Chutney
(recipe on page 15)

Orange-Cranberry Bread

Roasted New Potatoes with Garlic and Thyme

Spinach with Sautéed Mushrooms

Date-Walnut Pudding with
Ginger Sabayon Cream

Serves 6–8

Cream of Squash Soup

1 piece banana squash, 3½–4 lb (1.5–2 kg),
   cut into quarters and any seeds and
   strings removed
4–8 whole cloves
1 cup (8 fl oz/250 ml) boiling water
2 tablespoons unsalted butter
1 cup (5 oz/155 g) chopped yellow onion
½ teaspoon crushed dried marjoram
4 cups (32 fl oz/1 l) chicken stock,
   preferably homemade (recipe on page 13)
1 teaspoon fresh lemon juice
salt and freshly ground pepper
1 cup (8 fl oz/250 ml) heavy (double)
   cream
sour cream
freshly grated nutmeg or chopped fresh
   parsley or mint

Although banana squash is called for here, Hubbard or other large winter squash, including pumpkin, can be used. The soup can be prepared up to the point where the cream is added; cover and refrigerate for up to 24 hours, then finish just before serving. Any leftover soup can be put in a bowl, covered and refrigerated until the next day, then reheated slowly. Decoratively cut green (spring) onion makes an extra-festive garnish.

★

Preheat an oven to 375°F (190°C).

Stick 1 or 2 whole cloves in the flesh of each squash piece. Place the pieces flesh-side down in a baking pan or ovenproof dish. Pour in the boiling water. Place in the oven and bake until tender when the flesh is pierced, about 1 hour, adding additional boiling water if the pan begins to dry. Remove from the oven and leave the squash in the pan until cool, 20–25 minutes. Discard the cloves and scoop out the flesh; you should have about 5 cups (2½ lb/1.25 kg). Set aside.

In a large saucepan over low heat, melt the butter. Add the onion and marjoram, cover and cook over very low heat until translucent and tender, 15–20 minutes. Remove from the heat.

In a food processor fitted with the metal blade, combine the squash and onion-marjoram mixture. Process to a smooth purée. Return the purée to the saucepan and stir in the stock and lemon juice. Cook over medium-low heat, stirring frequently, to blend the flavors, 8–10 minutes. Do not allow to scorch. Season to taste with salt and pepper.

Just before serving, stir in the cream and heat almost to a boil. Ladle into soup bowls and top with a dollop of sour cream and a grating of nutmeg or a sprinkling of parsley or mint.

Serves 6–8 with leftovers

Roast Leg of Lamb

1 leg of lamb, 6–7 lb (3–3.5 kg), at room
   temperature
2 tablespoons dry mustard
2 tablespoons olive oil or vegetable oil
1 tablespoon chopped fresh rosemary or
   1 teaspoon crushed dried rosemary
salt and freshly ground pepper
½ cup (4 fl oz/125 ml) water, or as needed

For a good leg of lamb, seek out a specialty meat market or the butcher in the meat department of a quality supermarket. The flesh should be pink and not red. If possible, have the butcher remove the fell, or papery film that covers the fat, along with any excess fat. Remove the lamb from the refrigerator about 2 hours before cooking, to bring it to room temperature. Accompany with apple-mint chutney (recipe on page 15).

✴

Preheat an oven to 350°F (180°C). Position a rack in the lower third of the oven.

Remove the papery film and excess fat from the leg of lamb, if not done by the butcher. Wipe the lamb with a damp cloth. In a cup stir together the mustard, oil and rosemary to form a paste. Spread over the surface of the lamb. Sprinkle with salt and pepper and place on a flat rack in a roasting pan, fat-side up. Place in the oven and roast until browned and done as desired. Check for doneness by inserting an instant-read thermometer in the thickest part of the leg away from bone. It should register 135° (57°C) for pink. It will reach this point after about 1½ hours. See page 8 for temperatures for other degrees of doneness.

Transfer to a warmed platter. Cover loosely with aluminum foil and let rest until ready to carve, 10–15 minutes. Meanwhile, prepare the pan juices: Pour off just the fat from the roasting pan, leaving the pan juices. Heat the pan juices over medium heat. Add the water and deglaze the pan by stirring to dislodge any browned bits stuck to the pan. Bring to a boil and season to taste with salt and pepper. Add more water if needed to reach the desired consistency and taste.

Carve the lamb (see page 12) and serve with the pan juices in a bowl on the side.

Serves 6–8

Orange-Cranberry Bread

1½ cups (6 oz/185 g) fresh cranberries
grated zest of 1 orange
1 cup (8 oz/250 g) sugar
1½ cups (7½ oz/235 g) all-purpose (plain)
 flour
½ cup (2½ oz/75 g) yellow cornmeal
½ teaspoon salt
1½ teaspoons baking powder
½ teaspoon baking soda (bicarbonate of
 soda)
3 tablespoons unsalted butter, at room
 temperature
1 egg, lightly beaten
½ cup (4 fl oz/125 ml) fresh orange juice
½ cup (4 fl oz/125 ml) water

This bread can be made a day in advance, cooled, wrapped in plastic wrap or aluminum foil and stored at room temperature. In addition to roast lamb, this would be good served with roast turkey or chicken. Excellent for cold turkey sandwiches, too.

★

*P*reheat an oven to 325°F (165°C). Position a rack in the middle of the oven. Butter an 8½-by-4½-by-2½-inch (21-by-11-by-6-cm) loaf pan.

Sort the cranberries and discard any soft ones. Coarsely chop them and place in a small saucepan over low heat. Add the orange zest and ½ cup (4 oz/125 g) of the sugar and heat slowly just to a simmer, stirring to dissolve the sugar. Set aside to cool.

In a bowl stir together the flour, cornmeal, salt, baking powder and baking soda. Set aside.

In a separate bowl combine the butter and the remaining ½ cup (4 oz/125 g) sugar. Beat until light and fluffy, about 3 minutes. Beat in the egg. Stir in half of the flour mixture, and then the orange juice and water. Stir in the remaining flour mixture and then the cooled cranberry mixture. Do not overmix. Spoon the batter into the prepared loaf pan. Place in the oven and bake until a toothpick inserted in the center of the loaf comes out clean, 55–60 minutes.

Remove from the oven and let rest for 5 minutes. Turn out onto a wire rack and let cool. Slice and serve.

Makes 1 loaf; serves 6–8

Roasted New Potatoes with Garlic and Thyme

salt
2–2½ lb (1–1.25 kg) red new potatoes,
   1½–2 inches (4–5 cm) in diameter, cut
   in half crosswise
¼ cup (2 fl oz/60 ml) extra-virgin olive oil
4 or 5 garlic cloves, cut in half
1 tablespoon coarsely chopped fresh
   thyme or 2 teaspoons crushed dried
   thyme
freshly ground pepper
chopped fresh parsley

Substitute rosemary for the thyme, if you like. If you have coarse salt, this recipe benefits from its use. It is best to have two ovens in order to roast the potatoes and lamb at the same time. However, you can roast the potatoes in the 350°F (180°C) oven with the lamb, in which case you may need to increase the potatoes' cooking time slightly. Any leftover potatoes can be used to make a salad.

★

Preheat an oven to 375°F (190°C).

Fill a large pot three-fourths full with water and bring to a boil. Add 1 tablespoon salt and the potatoes. Bring back to a boil, reduce the heat slightly, cover partially and cook for 5 minutes. Drain well.

Arrange the potatoes in a baking dish or baking pan, preferably in a single layer. Drizzle the olive oil over the top, then turn the potatoes over several times so they are well coated with the oil. Sprinkle the garlic over the potatoes. Sprinkle on the thyme and a little salt and pepper.

Place in the oven and bake, turning the potatoes over several times, until tender and golden, 20–25 minutes.

Transfer to a serving dish, sprinkle with parsley and serve.

Serves 6–8

Spinach with Sautéed Mushrooms

3–4 bunches spinach, 2–2½ lb (1–1.25 kg)
1–1½ lb (500–750 g) fresh mushrooms
salt
freshly grated nutmeg
¼ cup (2 oz/60 g) unsalted butter
½ cup (3 oz/90 g) finely chopped yellow
   onion
2 lemons

Neither the spinach nor mushrooms can be cooked in advance, but they can be cleaned and trimmed up to 3 hours before cooking. The cooking is then very fast and simple. Look for mushrooms that are white and have tightly closed caps with no dark brown gills showing.

✳

Wash the spinach carefully and discard the stems and any tough outer leaves. Use 2 or 3 changes of water if necessary to rid the leaves of all sand. If cleaning spinach ahead of time, wrap in a damp towel and store in the refrigerator to crisp.

Clean the mushrooms by brushing off any dirt with a dry towel or mushroom brush. Cut into thick slices and set aside.

When ready to cook, drain the spinach and place in a large saucepan with only the water that clings to the leaves. Add 2 or 3 pinches of salt and a little nutmeg. Cover and cook over medium-high heat, turning the leaves a couple of times, until just wilted, about 2 minutes. Drain in a colander and press the leaves with the back of a spoon to remove all excess liquid. Return the spinach to the pan and fluff up the leaves. Cover partially and keep warm.

Melt the butter in a large sauté pan or frying pan over medium heat. Add the onion and cook gently until translucent, about 2 minutes. Add the mushrooms, raise the heat and stir and toss until just tender, 3–4 minutes. (Cook the mushrooms in two or more batches if the pan is not big enough to spread them out.) Season to taste with salt, nutmeg and a squeeze or so of lemon juice from 1 of the lemons. Toss well.

To serve, spoon the mushrooms into the center of a warmed shallow serving dish or platter. Surround with the spinach. Cut the remaining lemon into wedges for garnish.

Serves 6–8

Date-Walnut Pudding

½ cup (2½ oz/75 g) all-purpose (plain)
    flour
2 teaspoons baking powder
¼ teaspoon salt
1¼ cups (9 oz/280 g) firmly packed light
    brown sugar
3 eggs, at room temperature
½ cup (4 oz/125 g) unsalted butter, at
    room temperature
2 teaspoons finely grated orange zest
2 tablespoons dark rum
1½ cups (12 fl oz/375 ml) milk, at room
    temperature
1½ cups (12 oz/375 g) firmly packed,
    coarsely chopped pitted dates
1½ cups (6 oz/185 g) coarsely broken
    walnuts
extra dates and walnut halves for garnish
ginger sabayon cream (*recipe on page 19*)

Have the eggs, milk and butter at room temperature for this recipe. Select a baking dish that measures about 11½ by 8 by 2¼ inches (29 by 20 by 5.5 cm). If the dish is too large, the pudding will not be high enough and will bake too quickly. The pudding is best when baked just before serving, but do allow enough time for it to cool to warm.

★

Preheat an oven to 350°F (180°C). Position a rack in the middle of the oven. Generously butter a 2–2½-qt (2–2.5-l) earthenware, porcelain or heatproof-glass baking dish.

In a bowl stir together the flour, baking powder and salt. Set aside.

In another, larger bowl, combine the sugar and eggs. Using an electric mixer set on medium speed, beat until fluffy and thickened, about 3 minutes, scraping down the sides of the bowl at regular intervals. Add the butter and beat until well blended, another 3 minutes. Beat in the orange zest and the rum. Using a rubber spatula stir in the flour mixture and then beat in the milk. Stir in the dates and walnuts, being sure the date pieces are well distributed and not clinging to each other. The mixture will separate, but do not worry; it will come together during baking.

Pour the mixture into the prepared baking dish. Bake until golden brown and a knife inserted in the center comes out dry, 40–50 minutes. Remove from the oven and place on a wire rack. Garnish with the extra dates and walnut halves. Let cool slightly. Serve warm with ginger sabayon cream.

Serves 6–8 with leftovers

Glossary

The following glossary defines terms specifically as they relate to holiday menus, with a special emphasis on major and unusual ingredients.

ALLSPICE
Sweet spice of Caribbean origin with a flavor suggesting a blend of **cinnamon, clove** and **nutmeg,** hence its name. May be purchased as whole dried berries or ground.

APPLES
A variety of autumn and winter apples grace the holiday table. Among the most popular and widely available are Granny Smiths, an Australian variety ideal for cooking; pippins, green to yellow-green apples with a slightly tart taste suited to salads or cooking; red, slightly tart Rome apples, ideal for baking or eating raw; and red-and-green McIntoshes, good for eating raw or cooking.

AVOCADO
The finest-flavored variety of this popular fruit vegetable is the Haas, which has a pearlike shape and a thick, bumpy, dark green skin. Ripe, ready-to-use avocados will yield slightly to fingertip pressure. To remove the pit neatly, first, using a sharp knife, cut down to the pit lengthwise all around the avocado. Gently twist the halves in opposite directions to separate; lift away the half without the pit. Cup the half with the pit in the palm of one hand, with your fingers and thumb safely clear. Hold a sturdy, sharp knife with the other hand and strike the pit with the blade of the knife, wedging the blade firmly into the pit. Then twist and lift the knife to remove the pit.

BAKING POWDER
Commercial baking product combining three ingredients: **baking soda,** the source of the carbon dioxide that causes quick batters and doughs to rise; an acid, such as cream of tartar, calcium acid phosphate or sodium aluminum sulphate, which, when the powder is combined with a liquid, causes the baking soda to release its gas; and a starch such as cornstarch (cornflour) or flour, to keep the powder from absorbing moisture.

BAKING SODA
The active component of **baking powder** and the source of the carbon dioxide that leavens many baked goods. Often used on its own to leaven batters that include acidic ingredients such as buttermilk, yogurt or citrus juices. Also known as sodium bicarbonate or bicarbonate of soda.

BAY LEAVES
Dried whole leaves of the bay laurel tree. Pungent and spicy, they flavor simmered dishes, marinades and pickling mixtures. The French variety, sometimes available in specialty-food shops, has a milder, sweeter flavor than California bay leaves. Discard the leaves before serving.

BELL PEPPER
Fresh, sweet-fleshed, bell-shaped member of the pepper family. Also known as capsicum. Most common in the unripe green form, although ripened red or yellow varieties are also available. Creamy pale yellow, orange and purple-black types may also be found.

To prepare a raw bell pepper, cut it in half lengthwise with a sharp knife. Pull out the stem section from each half, along with the cluster of seeds attached to it. Remove any remaining seeds, along with any thin white membranes, or ribs, to which they are attached. Cut the pepper halves into quarters, strips or thin slices, as called for in the specific recipe.

To roast peppers: Place the peppers, resting on their sides, directly on the grid of a stove-top gas burner, or on a heavy wire rack placed over an electric stove-top burner (its feet resting on the stove top). Have gas flame on medium-high, or electric burner on high. Using metal tongs, turn the peppers over the heat until blackened, 5–6 minutes. Transfer

CHESTNUTS
Whole roasted peeled chestnuts or chestnut pieces are available in specialty-food shops and the specialty-food sections of markets. Raw chestnuts are sold encased in glossy brown shells that must be removed before use.

To Peel Chestnuts
1. Use a sharp knife to score an X in the shell on the flat side of each chestnut.

2. Put the chestnuts in a baking pan large enough to hold them in a single layer and place in a preheated 400°F (200°C) oven for about 15 minutes, until the shells begin to turn brittle and peel back at the X.

3. Peel off the brittle shells and the furry skin directly under them. Do not let the chestnuts cool or they will be difficult to peel.

Alternatively, immerse the chestnuts in boiling water to cover for about 5 minutes. Turn off the heat but leave the chestnuts in the water to keep them warm, to facilitate peeling. One at a time, peel the chestnuts.

peppers to a colander and place in a sink under cold running water. Using your hands, hold each pepper over the colander and under the running water and rub off the loosened, blackened skin. It will fall off easily. Dry peppers on paper towels, cut in half vertically and remove the core, seeds and ribs.

BIBB LETTUCE
Relatively small type of round lettuce with soft, loosely packed, tender, mildly flavored leaves. Also known as limestone lettuce. A member of the butterhead family, which also includes the Boston variety.

CAYENNE PEPPER
Very hot ground spice derived from dried cayenne chili peppers.

CHICORY
Also known as curly endive, this relative of Belgian endive has loosely packed, curly leaves characterized by their bitter flavor. The paler center leaves, or heart, of a head of chicory are milder than the dark green outer leaves.

CHUTNEY
Refers to any number of spiced East Indian–style relishes or pickles served as condiments with meals and used as seasonings in cooking; most common are fruit-based chutneys, particularly mango. Available in ethnic markets, specialty-food stores and in the Asian-food section of well-stocked food stores.

CINNAMON
Popular sweet spice used primarily for flavoring baked goods and desserts. The aromatic bark of a type of evergreen tree, it is sold as whole dried strips—cinnamon sticks—or ground.

CLOVE
Rich and aromatic East African spice used ground in baked goods and whole in pickling brines and as a seasoning for baked hams.

CORNMEAL
Granular flour, ground from the dried kernels of yellow or white corn, with a sweet, robust flavor that is particularly appealing in baked goods. Sometimes known by the Italian term *polenta*. Most commercial cornmeal sold in food stores lacks the kernel's husk and germ and is available in fine or coarser grinds. Stone-ground cornmeal, made from whole corn kernels, produces a richer flour.

CRANBERRIES
Round, deep red, tart berries, grown primarily in wet, sandy coastal lands—or bogs—in the northeastern United States. Available fresh during the late autumn, and frozen year-round. Dried cranberries, resembling raisins in shape, are also available in specialty-food stores, for use in baking or in sauces and chutneys.

CREAM, HEAVY
Heavy whipping cream with a butterfat content of at least 36 percent. For the best flavor and cooking properties, purchase fresh cream, avoiding long-lasting

HERBS, CRUSHING
To release their full flavor in dishes to which they are added, dried herbs often require crushing. This is easily done by rubbing them on the palm of your hand with the opposite thumb. For larger quantities, dried herbs may be rubbed through a wire-meshed sieve.

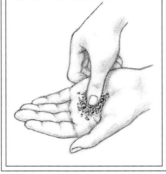

varieties that have been processed by ultraheat methods. In Britain use double cream.

CREAM, SOUR
Commercial dairy product made from pasteurized sweet cream, used as an enrichment in a wide range of savory and sweet recipes. Like buttermilk, its extra acidity boosts the leavening action of **baking soda** in quick breads.

DATES
Sweet, deep brown fruit of the date palm tree, with a thick, sticky consistency resembling that of candied fruit. Sometimes sold already pitted and chopped.

FENNEL STALKS, DRIED
The dried stalks of fennel, used as an herb to impart a mild anise flavor to savory or sweet dishes. Sometimes available in specialty-food shops.

FETA CHEESE
Crumbly textured Greek-style cheese made from goat's or sheep's milk, notable for its salty, slightly sharp flavor.

FLOUR, ALL-PURPOSE
The most common form of commercial flour, this bleached and blended (hard and soft wheats) variety is available in all food stores. Also called plain flour.

FRISÉE
A close relative of **chicory** (curly endive) but with a more delicate flavor and slightly more tender leaves. The pale green leaves with spiky edges form a loose head.

GINGER
The rhizome of the tropical ginger plant, which yields a sweet, strong-flavored spice. Whole ginger rhizomes, commonly but mistakenly called roots, may be purchased fresh in a well-stocked food store or vegetable market. Ginger pieces are available crystallized or candied in specialty-food shops or food-store baking sections, or preserved in syrup in specialty shops or Asian food sections. Ground, dried ginger is easily found in jars or tins in the food-store spice section.

GREEN BEANS, BLUE LAKE
Variety of fresh green bean, or string bean, particularly prized for its small size, bright color, fresh flavor and crisp texture. Substitute any other variety of fresh green bean.

HONEY

The natural, sweet, syruplike substance produced by bees from flower nectar, honey subtly reflects the color, taste and aroma of the blossoms from which it was made. Milder varieties, such as clover and orange blossom, are lighter in color and better suited to general cooking purposes. Those derived from herb blossoms, such as **thyme**, have a more distinctively aromatic taste.

HORSERADISH

Pungent, hot-tasting root, a member of the mustard family, sold fresh and whole, or already grated and bottled as a prepared sauce. The best prepared horseradish is the freshly grated variety, bottled in a light vinegar and found in the refrigerated section of the food store.

LENTILS

Small, disk-shaped dried legumes, prized for their rich, earthy flavor when cooked.

MADEIRA

Sweet, amber dessert wine originating on the Portuguese island of Madeira.

MARJORAM

Pungent, aromatic herb used dried or fresh to season meats (particularly lamb), poultry, seafood, vegetables and eggs.

MINT

Refreshing sweet herb used fresh or dried to flavor lamb, poultry, vegetables and fruits.

MUSTARD

Dijon mustard is made in Dijon, France, from dark brown mustard seeds (unless otherwise marked *blanc*) and white wine or wine vinegar. Pale, fairly hot and sharp tasting, true Dijon mustard and non-French blends labeled "Dijon-style" are widely available in food stores. Dry mustard is an intensely hot powder ground from mustard seeds.

NUTMEG

Popular baking spice that is the hard pit of the fruit of the nutmeg tree (below). May be bought already ground or, for fresher flavor, whole.

OIL, OLIVE

Extra-virgin olive oil, extracted from olives on the first pressing without use of heat or chemicals, is preferred for salads and other dishes in which its fruity taste is desired. Many brands, varying in color and strength of flavor, are now available; choose one that suits your taste. The higher-priced extra-virgin olive oils usually are of better quality. Oils simply labeled "olive oil" (the results of subsequent pressings) are good for sautéing, frying and other cooking purposes. Store all olive oils in airtight containers away from heat and light.

ONIONS

All manner of onions are used to enhance the rich flavor of savory dishes. Green onions (shown at right), also called spring onions or scallions, are a variety harvested immature, leaves and all, before their bulbs have formed; the green and white parts may both be enjoyed, raw or cooked, for their mild but still pronounced onion flavor. Red (Spanish) onions are a mild, sweet variety of onion with

SPINACH

Choose small, tender spinach leaves if possible. Be sure to wash thoroughly to eliminate all dirt and sand.

To remove tough stems from mature leaves, fold the leaf in half, glossy side in. Grasp the stem and pull it toward the leaf tip, peeling it off the leaf.

Put the spinach leaves in a sink or large basin and fill with cold water to cover them thoroughly. Agitate the leaves in the water to remove their dirt. Then lift the leaves out of the water and set aside.

Drain the sink or basin thoroughly and rinse out all dirt and sand. Repeat the above procedure until no grit remains.

purplish red skin and red-tinged white flesh. Yellow onions are the common, white-fleshed, strong-flavored variety distinguished by their dry, yellowish brown skins. Small but pungent pearl onions, less than 1 inch (2.5 cm) in diameter, and small white boiling onions, about 1 inch in diameter, are often cooked as side dishes in their own right, as well as being added whole to stews and braises and used for pickling.

PAPRIKA

Powdered spice derived from the dried paprika pepper; popular in several European cuisines and available in sweet, mild and hot forms. Hungarian paprika is the best, but Spanish paprika, which is mild, may also be used. Buy in small quantities from shops with a high turnover, to ensure a fresh, flavorful supply.

PARSLEY

This widely used fresh herb is available in two varieties, the more popular curly-leaf type and a flat-leaf type. The latter, also known as Italian parsley, has a more pronounced flavor and is preferred.

PARSNIPS

Root vegetable similar in shape and texture to the carrot, but with ivory flesh and an appealingly sweet flavor.

POLENTA
See cornmeal.

PUMPKIN
See squashes.

ROSEMARY
Mediterranean herb, used either fresh or dried, with a strong aromatic flavor well suited to lamb, veal and poultry. Strong in flavor, it should be used sparingly, except when grilling.

SAGE
Pungent herb, used either fresh or dried, that goes particularly well with fresh or cured pork, lamb, veal or poultry.

SHORTENING, VEGETABLE
Solid vegetable fat sometimes used in place of or in combination with butter in doughs. The fat is said to "shorten" the flour, that is, to make it flaky and tender.

SQUASHES
The pale yellow to deep orange flesh of hard, tough-skinned winter squashes such as acorn, banana, butternut, Hubbard or pumpkin makes a colorful, flavorful ingredient for holiday soups, side dishes and desserts.

Banana Squash

While canned unsweetened pumpkin purée is available in food markets and may be substituted for the cooked and mashed vegetable, other winter squashes require cooking and mashing for use in recipes.

SUGAR, BROWN
A rich, fine-textured granulated sugar combined with molasses in varying quantities to yield light or dark varieties. Widely available in baking sections of food stores.

SUGAR, CONFECTIONERS'
Finely pulverized form of sugar, also known as powdered or icing sugar, which dissolves very quickly.

SUGAR, DEMERARA
See raw sugar.

SUGAR, RAW
Sugar labeled "raw" is not true raw sugar, which contains too many impurities to be sold. What is labeled as raw sugar is a coarse, brownish, partially refined product that still contains the natural molasses present in sugarcane. Either turbinado sugar—coarse amber crystals that have been treated with steam to remove impurities—or demerara sugar, which is commonly found in Britain and is more highly refined than turbinado sugar, can be used in recipes calling for raw sugar.

SWEET POTATOES
Form of vegetable tuber similar in shape and consistency to potatoes, to which it is not related, but with a distinctively sweet, yellow flesh.

SWISS CHARD
Also known as chard or silverbeet, a leafy dark green vegetable with thick, crisp white or red stems and ribs. The green part, often trimmed from the stems and ribs, may be cooked like **spinach**, and has a somewhat milder flavor.

THYME
Fragrant, clean-tasting, small-leaved herb popular fresh or dried as a seasoning for poultry, light meats, seafood or vegetables. A variety called lemon thyme imparts a pleasant lemon scent to foods.

TOMATOES
During summer, when tomatoes are in season, red or yellow sun-ripened tomatoes are preferable. At other times of year, however, plum tomatoes, sometimes called Roma or egg tomatoes, are likely to have the best flavor and texture.

VINEGAR
Literally "sour" wine, vinegar results when certain strains of yeast cause wine—or some other alcoholic liquid such as apple cider or rice wine—to ferment for a second time, turning it acidic. The best-quality wine vinegars begin with good-quality wine. French Champagne vinegar, for example, displays the delicate flavor of that sparkling wine. Flavored vinegars are made by adding herbs such as tarragon and dill or fruits such as raspberries.

WATER CHESTNUTS
Walnut-sized bulbs of an Asian plant grown in water, with brown skins concealing a refreshingly crisp, slightly sweet white flesh. Most often sold in cans already peeled and sometimes sliced or chopped, water chestnuts are occasionally found fresh in Asian markets.

WATERCRESS
Refreshing, slightly peppery, dark green leaf vegetable commercially cultivated and also found wild in freshwater streams. Used primarily in salads and as a popular garnish.

ZEST
Thin, brightly colored, outermost layer of a citrus fruit's peel, containing most of its aromatic essential oils—a lively source of flavor. Zest may be removed using one of two easy methods:

1. Use a simple tool known as a zester, drawing its sharp-edged holes across the fruit's skin to remove the zest in thin strips. Alternatively, use a fine-holed hand-held grater.

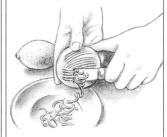

2. Holding the edge of a paring knife or vegetable peeler away from you and almost parallel to the fruit's skin, carefully cut off the zest in thin strips, taking care not to remove any white pith with it. Then thinly slice or chop on a cutting board.

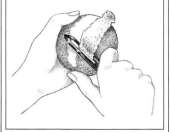

Index

ACKNOWLEDGMENTS

The publishers would like to thank the following people and organizations for their generous assistance and support in producing this book:
Elaine Anderson, Sharon C. Lott, Stephen W. Griswold, James Obata, Tara Brown, Ken DellaPenta, the buyers for Gardener's Eden,
and the buyers and store managers for Pottery Barn and Williams-Sonoma stores.

The following kindly lent props for the photography:
Candelier, Louis D. Fenton Antiques, J. Goldsmith Antiques, Green Valley Growers, Stephanie Greenleigh, Sue Fisher King, Cynthia and Edward MacKay,
Karen Nicks, Lorraine and Judson Puckett, Waterford Wedgwood (San Francisco), Sue White and Chuck Williams.